Outside Eden

Essays of Encouragement

By Peter Short

The United Church

Observer

Published by Observer Publications Inc.

Outside Eden: *Essays of Encouragement*

Copyright © 2006 by Peter Short

Published in 2006 by Observer Publications Inc.
478 Huron St.,
Toronto, ON
M5R 2R3
Tel. 416-960-8500
Fax 416-960-8477
www.ucobserver.org

Library and Archives Canada Cataloguing in Publication

Short, Peter, 1948-
Outside Eden: Essays of Encouragement / written by Peter Short.

ISBN 0-9780768-0-X

1. Trust in God. 2. Christian life. I. Title.

BT103.S56 2006   231
C2006-901903-7

For Sue

I'll be looking at the moon
But I'll be seeing you.

VI   OUTSIDE EDEN

Table of Contents

VIII   OUTSIDE EDEN

Foreword

The United Church Observer publishes magazines, not books. When we assign articles, we resist any notion that they should approach book length. Yet we came to believe that the United Church and beyond would be better for having a collection of the writing of Peter Short between two covers. Here it is – six already-published pieces, eight new.

We didn't even know he could write when he was elected as The United Church of Canada's 38th moderator in 2003. But we soon learned that Peter Short writes exceedingly well and he has something significant to say. His articles in *The Observer* – on Easter, on the Middle East, on Jesus' work of tears – quickly won reader acclaim and church-press awards. "Highly original and deeply engaging," wrote one impressed judge.

Short sees our lives, our beliefs, our falling down and our fragile hopes from enough distance to give us perspective, but from close enough to convince us he has been here too.

He loves mystery. He delights in the elusive God who hides in thick darkness, the one who never lets us go. He is content with a God who cannot be explained, but who will explain us, if we wait with a good heart.

Freedom is essential to Peter Short. He never tells his readers what to think, never talks down to us. So each of us finds in his work a different landscape, according to the season of our need. It is intellectual and imaginative, requiring our whole attention. It is exhilarating and compelling. The strength of Short's language and the compassion that fills it will induce you to read this book eagerly to the end, and then start over.

By that time, you may know some things about your God, maybe about your church, and certainly about yourself that you hadn't known before.

Muriel Duncan and Donna Sinclair
The United Church Observer

Acknowledgements

"Imitation is the sincerest of flattery."

It is also how we learn. Imitation is how we learn to drive a car or a nail. I learned to print words in the first grade by imitating Miss Farlinger. I learned to write them from a great community of the quick and the dead. Among the many I imitate are Frederick Buechner and Annie Dillard. I am grateful for their writing labours, though I've not had the privilege of meeting either. I have had the privilege of spending time at table, in conversation and in song, with William Sloane Coffin Jr., whose presence and hand can be seen everywhere in this work, borrowings too numerous to name.

I am indebted to Nora Sanders, Elaine Stewart, Sue Short, Marie Wilson and Donna Allen, northern soul sisters, who long ago encouraged me. I think I might have flown too close to the sun without Ian Fraser, Paul Scott, Frank Giffen, Paul Evans and the group that gathered every Thursday to enter the mysteries of Scripture and of friendship. Too close to the sun or too deep in the darkness – there's not much difference in the end. Jim Sinclair helped me get started 30 years ago and is a faithful mentor to this day.

It has been a blessing to work with sages and trusted guides Donna Sinclair and Muriel Duncan of *The United Church Observer*. They are admired writers in their own right. I am grateful to the board of the *Observer* for believing, and to Linda McNamara for making things possible.

My beloved family has never once intimated that I was unworthy of the ministry that has been my life, though God knows I gave them cause often enough. I thank them each one: Greg, Christine, Emily, Robert and Sue. My grandmother Lillian, long gone, is with me yet – stargazer and exotic friend to a child.

Peter Short
Fredericton, New Brunswick
Lent, 2006

Introduction

In the beginning ... God created the heavens and the earth. (Gen.1.1)

THE BIBLE INFORMS YOU in its first 10 words that you live in a creation, that you *are* a creation. Someone has willed you to be, no less than the trees and the stars.

This is all it really means to be a believer. It is to realize that you've been snatched out of oblivion by life. You don't have life, life has you. You can't have an approach to life, as if life were something that can be approached at all. Where would you be approaching it from?

No, somehow life has got hold of you through no great accomplishment of your own. Life has set you down in the landscape you find yourself in right now. In case you don't know where you are today, you are in a land the Bible calls *east of Eden*, which is another way of saying, no paradise. The ancient writings will also tell you that the way back to the garden is barred by an angel with a flaming sword.

You may not be able to get back to the garden, but the residual memory of paradise remains, lingering like a scent of jasmine in the air. You are a paradise-haunted creature. If it were not so – paradise lost – why ever would you expect so much of the world? Why would you expect so much of yourself? See how you rage at greed and injustice and the desecration of the good earth. Count the ways in which you've known all over again that this world is no paradise.

But it *ought* to be, dammit! And that relentless *"ought"* is the clue. That powerful *"it ought to be"* is nothing less than the insurrection of the subjugated knowledge of Eden.

So here you are outside the garden – you and your checkered past, you and your foolish dreams. Many of your dreams are broken, yes, but dreams all the same. Imagine. At your age you've still the capacity to generate them, dreams I mean. Dreams get into your soul in spite of yourself and in spite of all the evidence. Dreams point to the wild presence of hope, one of the great gifts of the Spirit.

The opening sentence of the Bible proclaims all this. God created. That is not a geophysical explanation. It's not creationist science. It's not any science at all. It's proclamation. God's world! In the beginning God created the heavens and the earth. God enchanted! God haunted!

It's a creation too vast and too intimate to be comprehended by the mental calculations of the brain. There are so many mountains of data to climb and so many tiny seeds of mystery to hold in the palm of the hand.

In *For the Time Being*, Annie Dillard, describing the billions of galaxies in the incomprehensible immensity of creation, passes through the veil from data to meaning:

Two galaxies, nine galaxies . . . one hundred billion suns, four hundred billion suns . . . twelve billion years, thirteen billion years . . .

These astronomers are nickel-and-diming us to death . . .

Does anyone believe that the galaxies exist to add splendour to the night sky over Bethlehem?

She asks a good question. Does anyone believe in the midst of all the data? Does anyone dare to imagine that the stars might be distant bright sisters casting splendour into the night over Bethlehem?

God help Bethlehem, it could use some splendour. It has a 15-metre-high concrete wall around it. One way in, one way out. You have to have a permit to pass. O Bethlehem, you are no paradise.

Does anyone believe that the galaxies exist to bless Bethlehem with glory in the night?

As a matter of fact, children do. Children know instinctively that everything has a meaning and that everything has a place in the economy of wonder and that the stars have a job to do. So if you ask a small child why the stars come out at night, she will tell you why – because the moon is afraid of the dark or because a ship needs to find its way across the wide, dark sea.

If you ask adults why the stars come out at night, we'll give you facts masquerading as knowledge, data drained of meaning, billions of numbers until your mind is nickel-and-dimed to death. Adults know the facts of optics: the stars don't *come out* at all. The stars are always there, though undetected by the human eye in the presence of ambient daylight. Adults can tell you how the stars come out at night but we can't tell you *why*. We don't know anymore. We've lost the thread of why.

Maybe the stars come out to say to earth's sister and brother creatures, *Don't be afraid.* Maybe the stars come out for people who long to come out too – little dark stars longing to come out and shine in God's heaven like all the others.

I hope that this book will in some humble way encourage you to venture out under God's stars. I want to tell you what I've found: that there is something wild about the presence we name God; that we don't explain God, God explains us; that we live in a meaning-riddled world but meaning can't be managed; that there is a victory to belong to if we can rid ourselves of the addiction to winning; and that there is a presence in the soul that speaks to us of home.

This book is ultimately about encouragement because, after all, the world needs your precious life – all of it. Not just your brain with its data but all of your life, including the part that listens to the stars and is haunted by the memory of Eden. We are anxious to hear from you and to be blessed by you because our minds are nickel-and-dimed to death. The world longs for brave and dreaming creatures who will walk the dark streets of our Bethlehems and never lose sight of the splendour.

The Bible could have started in any number of ways but it began with the words, *In the beginning when God created the heavens and the earth. . . .* I think I know why. It began there because of where people find themselves ending up. The beginning sentence is there to remind you that when you know your beginning is in God, no matter where you've ended up you can always go home.

This is not to say that going home is easy. Ever since Luke wrote his Gospel, we've known of an older brother who hates the grace of home and who stands resentful in the way – another angel with a flaming sword. Yet behind him there is a distant sound, one familiar to ear and heart. Sometimes it can be heard above the roaring of the angel with the flaming sword. It is the sound of music. There is music in the father's house.

This book is a way of speaking about home. But it is also about a passage through territory belonging to a wild mystery. They go together, the wild mystery and home, though they will not be reconciled. This is how it is outside the garden under the stars.

Patience

Tears in a Bottle

> *You have kept count of my*
> > *tossings;*
> > *put my tears in your bottle.*
> > *Are they not in your record?*
> (Psalm 56:8)

MY FIRST LOVE HELD ME (well, carried me really) in her arms at the dance. She was beautiful beyond describing and I was far too happy to be aware of happiness. I could have danced all night. I was four years old. Then one day, the unimaginable – she got married. I cried. I had no idea then that someone saved the tears in a bottle.

Many years later I would learn the words of a lament that calls out to the deep:

> *You have kept count of my*
> > *tossings;*
> > *put my tears in your bottle.*

A young immigrant woman, poor, had come to the church to say that her mother was dying in a country overseas. She could not go to be with her mother, so she had come to ask, "Can we pray for her?" As we prayed she wept. When we had finished praying, she sat quietly for a while. Then she thanked me and left.

Next morning, a knock at the door of the church study; a woman entered and said, "You don't know me, I go to the Pentecostal Church, but I have been led here to see you." I invited her to sit. She told me that every week she gave money for the work of her church. But every week she also set aside some of her gift as a reserve for when the Spirit came. She never knew when or where it might happen, but she knew the Spirit was near because of the tears. When the tears came she would stop, wherever she happened to be, and in the interior stillness she would await the Spirit's guidance. "Today," she said, "the tears came. They led me to you."

She opened her purse and handed me a sheaf of bills – a thousand dollars. She said, "I don't know what this money is for, but you will know." Then she rose and left. She hadn't told me her name.

In the luminous moment when the door closed behind her, I came to see that the tears of this unusual visitor were responding to the tears of the one who wept for her mother. When I arranged for the money to get to the young woman (not saying where it had come from), her tears came again. They were those inexplicable ones drawn at once from the well of happiness and the well of sadness.

put my tears in your bottle

Brenda's nine-year-old son died last week. She came into the church office to leave a card for the organist and to see if we could use the boy's toys. We could. She was glad and she smiled. But her chin quivered.

Sheila had a fight with Phil. She wants to "put him in the court for spousal assault." She has a black eye and a bruised arm. She has allies ("the legal aid") but the police jailed her instead of him. Who knows what really happened? She says he's out drinking now.

Her chin quivers when she talks. How many women are living with quivering chins? Children? Men?

put my tears in your bottle

Two rows ahead on the plane there is a woman who is weeping. The flight attendant is at her side asking if he can help. She talks quietly with him, hunched over, saying she is afraid to fly. He reassures her and lets her know that she can call him at any time. His compassionate manner quiets her, but then as he leaves to go about other duties she starts crying all the more. He returns to her to see what has happened. She tells him she is crying because she is embarrassed. She is ashamed to cry in the plane, with all these people.

Memories surface, memories of inoculations at school. I fear the needle, but even more I fear that I might cry. The agony is in the anticipation – the line-up in the school gym. I am watching the kids in front of me, listening for the sobs. The girl ahead of me faints. I step up. Oowee! But look – no tears! I make it through. No tears. I think it's great – no tears. I think it's great not to cry.

put my tears in your bottle

One night, deep in the watches, a call came from the hospital. Could I come? A woman had "lost" her baby. I dressed and went. She was lying in a strange calm in her room. The nurses were just bringing in the still child. It was a girl. The nurses, through their own tears, had dressed her in white and put a little striped cap on her head. Now they were laying the child on her mother's stomach. She stroked the tiny form and said, "Her name is Rose – for her grandmother." Together, we wept out the words of eternal life over the child, over ourselves, over the bewildering darkness upon the face of the deep. Rose.

put my tears in your bottle

This is my first appointment with the counsellor. I sit in the waiting room pretending to read a magazine. Like the line-up in the school gym of old, the agony is in the anticipation. Someone has called my name. I walk resolutely toward the sound of her voice, trying for all the world not to cry. She indicates a chair blessed by morning sunshine from a tall window. As I talk to her, I see tears in the sunlight on her face. At first I think she is overwhelmed by the poignancy of my tale or, more probably, burned out from listening day after day to so much human sadness, anger, and regret.

Slowly, I become aware that the tears are her work. I have known others like her. Usually they weep in odd times and places, without knowing why or for whom. They are God's spies – like crazy old Lear and brave young Cordelia – taking upon themselves the mystery of things. I think the mystery is a web of underground compassion. Some people have the gift for it, for the inexplicable tears.

> You have kept count of my
>   tossings;
> put my tears in your bottle.
> Are they not in your record?

HOW DO THE TEARS GET IN THE BOTTLE?
That is Jesus work.

The work of Jesus is a sort of opposite to the work of, say, Johnny Appleseed who walks up and down in the landscape sowing seeds. Jesus goes through the world collecting tears. This is called "Incarnation" by the theologians. It means God's presence in human form. I have heard the Incarnation described as "a flickering." This is a way of saying that God's gift of Christ among us is not a continuous status. It occurs in moments such as the moment when the Samaritan stops on the road and bends down to tend to the man in the ditch.

This is Christ, present in the moment of a human life. God, the flickering.

Maybe the Incarnation is a flickering. Would it be the same to say that it is a quivering – a quivering of the chin?

John announced the Incarnation right at the beginning of his Gospel. He called it a glory: *And the Word became flesh and lived among us, and we have seen his glory, the glory as of a father's only son, full of grace and truth.* (John 1:14)

Later on, closer to the cross, John would describe the Incarnation more succinctly: *Jesus wept.* (John 11:35)

> *You have kept count of my*
> > *tossings;*
> > *put my tears in your bottle.*
> > *Are they not in your record?*

Yes, they are.

Freed from Illusion

If we could be twice young and twice old we could correct all our mistakes.

    – Euripides

I DOUBT IT. If given a second chance at life I suspect I would make a lot of the same mistakes all over again. After all, experience is not the same thing as wisdom, and character is never possessed, only enacted.

But the point the philosopher makes is that I won't get the chance to be twice young and twice old. I cannot return to any time in my life – no going back to avoid the blunder that has left its scar; no taking back the careless word that flew out before I thought.

That's how it is for all of us. Do you realize that you have never before been the age you are now and you will never be this age again? You are learning it as you go. Which is another way of saying that you are forever growing up.

Often when we say "growing up" we mean becoming an adult. I mean more than that. I mean growing an appreciation for the complexity and the mystery of life. I mean living more deeply from the soul, and living on more intimate terms with the odd and terrible and wonderful truth of things.

In this sense, growing up is happening to us all, right now, no matter how many miles have crept onto the odometer while we weren't looking. No matter how many Christmases we have seen. If growing up means moving to a greater maturity, we are always growing up. Or failing to grow up. Or refusing.

A person can get lost growing up or swept away by the tides or changed by the power of a dream. There is terror, exhilaration, disappointment and wild hope. Part of what makes growing up such a precarious passage is that it will not happen without our being disillusioned; that is, to have our illusions destroyed. The emotions of disillusion are sadness, regret and anger.

Ministers know these emotions. So does a parent. And the one filling in another job application. In the end, no one escapes disillusion; for we all have set out with banners flying in pursuit of some dream.

But here's the thing: the end of an illusion is a liberation as well. Maybe it's an uninvited liberation and unwanted, but a liberation all the same. Ready or not, the end of an illusion opens the door to a deeper truth and into the unmanageable mysteries of a newly revealed world. And that's what this is all about: what to do when the illusions that had been trusted companions lie dead in the hills. Because at heart, that's what Christmas is all about.

Do you remember when, as a child, you found out about Santa Claus? You found old Santa out? That jolly wizard, that old impostor who taps away in his workshop at the North Pole or sits behind the great wheezing machine at the end of the yellow brick road? Were you disillusioned? Probably. Were you growing up? Yes. Did you come to distrust Christmas and to speak scornfully of its traditions and its dreams? It depends on what you did with your disillusionment. You were growing up. Still are after all these years.

The end of illusion opens an unexpected door that leads down a dark and unfamiliar stairway. The end of illusion takes you down into a world whose mystery cannot be managed and whose landscape is infinitely more demanding and astounding. Here you will encounter a new guide – a Spirit we have learned to call holy.

How odd of God to lead us down the dark stairway to a rude stable when we had been wishing the great innkeeper of heaven would prepare a place for us in the sky. How dark and backward, this animal shelter, when we had been expecting to see God at the high balconies of heaven. How unglorious, ungodlike.

For my thoughts are not your thoughts, nor are your ways my ways, says the Lord.(Is. 55:7-9)

And this will be a sign for you: you will find a babe wrapped in swaddling cloths and lying in a feed bin.

And because this is God's inexplicable beckoning down the dark stairway, you have to adjust your eyes to the dimness. You have to swallow your disappointment at the tattered squalor of it.

But after the unwelcome liberation you get new eyes. There is miracle happening right inside you. You are growing eyes to see a presence in the desperate places of human struggle; a presence that gives a new meaning to the word "holy." Here, at the end of illusion, you learn that in this life if you win it all and don't learn how to love, you have nothing.

All this is in the sacred story of Bethlehem, the one we know so well and are afraid to know so well.

This is why we must be at the business of growing up. The illusions won't hold. And the more desperate the struggle to keep them alive, the more they appear comical and then poignant and finally ghastly.

No, this Christmas you must arise and be on your way to find the presence. There is news of this presence and although it may take some time for you to get over the disappointment of it, it is news of great joy. For unto you is born a Saviour and this will be a sign for you. You will find a babe wrapped in rags and lying amongst the animals.

God, it is strange how you make us grow up. God, it is demanding how you call us to love. God, it is astounding how your thoughts are not our thoughts or our ways your ways. God, how it is good news that you did not after all fulfil our wishes and fantasies. You had something harder and better in store. Something more like you. And at the bottom, a presence. Joy.

When You Are
the Black Angel

WHEN I WAS GROWING UP, angels did not come in black. In fact, they didn't come in brown or yellow or red, either. Where I grew up, angels came in one colour. White. Everything about them was white: white robe, white crown, white aura, white skin. It has taken me a long time to realize that white angels are the offspring of white culture.

At the Christmas party we were singing carols. I found myself singing alongside a young woman named Choice Okoro. She was singing with much enthusiasm and delight: "I'm dreaming of a black Christmas." Choice is from Nigeria.

We are familiar enough with the inherited associations: white and light represent the good and the pure. Black and dark represent the sinister and the evil. We didn't mean the metaphors to extend to people and the colour of their skin. Really, we never meant it to be that way. When we sing about white Christmas, we mean snow, not skin. Choice knows that. But she knows too that for her own sake and for the sake of her small son, she must never stop dreaming of a black Christmas.

The metaphors through which we imagine the world are forever dying and rising. Sometimes, old ones are born again: *Moses drew near to the thick darkness where God was.* (Exodus 20:21)

To some, these sensitivities to language and metaphor seem silly. But a generation ago we began the painful and hopeful passage toward a verbal landscape that welcomed the footprint of woman. That, in its own hard and wondrous way, was a drawing near to the thick darkness where God was. The dark "blooms and sings," says the poet Wendell Berry; and it is "travelled by dark feet and dark wings."

Yet all of that is not why I want to tell about the black angel. The black angel is actually a white-skinned woman wearing a black turtleneck sweater. But I'm getting ahead of myself.

I have seen a lot of Christmas pageants and plays. Mostly, these dramas are organized by adults, acted by children.

I remember one such pageant. Entering the church on a brilliant December morning, I could see right away that the sanctuary had undergone pageant transformation. Stained-glass windows were covered with garbage bags to keep out the light so that you could read PowerPoint text on a screen. A coat hanger wrapped in silver garland hung high on the wall behind the pulpit (this was the star). Battery-powered candles in tall brass candelabras stood about the chancel. Here and there I caught glimpses of small people in bathrobes, disappearing around corners. Dads could be seen leaning against the side walls, camcorders at the ready. The congregation buzzed with the expectancy that is prelude to these things.

The adult choir opened with a spirited rendition of Prepare Ye The Way Of The Lord. That was the last we saw of that choir. The rest of this morning would belong to choirs of angels and to all the children about to take up their roles in a very adult drama.

The pageant was proceeding famously. The shepherds appeared on cue. The wise men arrived with a certain gravitas, counting some girls in their number. There was an innkeeper. Joseph was a strong and capable 12-year-old. He vowed to protect Mary from all danger. Mary, a little younger, told Joseph she loved him. She didn't giggle.

She was strong and capable, too.

By the fifth scene it was time for the angel to announce to the shepherds that there would be a holy birth. A seven-year-old girl angel popped up from her hiding place behind the pulpit – white gown, sparkly halo, wide grin. She looked out at the sea of adult faces, her eyes grew wide, a look of terror swept across her face and she disappeared behind the pulpit.

There is a long pause. Everyone is quiet. Negotiations behind the pulpit. We wait.

Eventually a woman stands up behind the pulpit where she too had been hiding. It is clear that she is one of the moms who coach and prompt and make costumes and dry tears. She is wearing a black turtleneck sweater. "We have a case of stage fright," she tells us. "I'll be the angel – the black angel."

Then she speaks the words that the angel must say in order for the drama to proceed. "Do not be afraid. See, I bring you good news of great joy." These are the words the seven-year-old would have said had she not been overcome by the moment. The black angel says the words because she has to say them in order to keep things going. The shepherds must receive their instruction to go to Bethlehem. The show must go on. Other children are waiting expectantly, not to mention the dads with the camcorders.

When spoken by the black angel, I hear the words as I have never heard them before, though I've heard them a thousand times and know them by heart. *Good news of great joy.* The same words conferred upon me through the years by an array of angels in white gowns and sparkly crowns and a tooth missing in the smile. "Don't be afraid . . . great joy . . . for all the people . . . born this day . . . a Saviour."

Something is different about the words this time. It is just so odd to hear the black angel saying these things. She is, after all, an adult. Surely she must know about the sham and the drudgery and the broken dreams of the world in which she finds herself an unlikely herald. Surely she knows of the exhaustion and hopelessness that overwhelms us. Surely she is aware that the world to which she announces the good news of a saviour is the very same planet that is sick to death with HIV/AIDS. "Great joy . . . for all the people . . . born this day . . ." Out of the mouths of babes the words have a certain sentimental appeal. But this is one of the black angels, one of the adults who know. One of us.

Here's what I'm saying to you this Christmas, while you sit and watch the pageant and think your own odd thoughts: you will know the meaning when you become the black angel. You will know the meaning when life sets you suddenly on the stage and bids you to say what you never in your wildest dreams thought you'd hear yourself saying – as if it were some other voice, some older, deeper, wilder voice. You will know the meaning when, in spite of all you've seen, you become the bearer of joy.

Yes, you can bear joy and you must, because this is God's world and all the teeming, reeling life this world contains is God's pageant. All the tragic and beautiful life this world lives is God's pageant, and when an angel misses her cue, you must step up to your part. The show must go on. Somehow it will not be complete without you; you, the bearer of joy. God alone knows why this is true. God alone knows why the word is to be conceived and brought to birth by the likes of you – the black angel.

It is clear to me now why we always give this profoundly demanding drama to the children to act out; give it to them while they still have the capacity for wonder. Give it to them before they drink too deep of the broken dreams. Give it to them while the heart is young, while they still sing as they skip on the sidewalk and still dream as they climb the tree. Give it to them because we have lost something of ourselves: good news of great joy.

Did you know that joy is not a mood? If you think joy is a good mood, you've been reading too much pop psychology and not enough sacred writings. A mood is something you may have but joy is something you can only belong to.

Joy is not a good mood, it is a good truth: a truth that lies deep in the heart of things. Joy is folded like a garment placed by a loving hand at the bottom of the drawer that is your soul. Joy is the strange knowledge that, in spite of all we have become and failed to become, we are born anew in Christ who is born to raise the daughters and sons of earth.

We don't have to make joy happen. We couldn't, even if we wanted to. Joy has been given. It is already true. Who will reach to the bottom of the drawer and bring it forth? The black angel.

When you are true to yourself, you become the black angel. This is what you must make of Christmas. You are no longer a child. Now this is what Christmas must make of you.

When I was growing up I never knew that angels could come in black. Now I know. I'm dreaming of a black Christmas because the one that travels on dark feet and dark wings has haunted this life with an insistent summons to joy.

There's Heaven
in This Ground

DO YOU THINK ABOUT HEAVEN? I know it's an odd question, but does heaven ever occur to you when you're standing at the corner waiting for the light to change or at the sink, staring out the window? Occasionally, does heaven send stray beams across your day or into your night? Ever?

Are you one who, when you get to thinking about God's territory, think of it as "up" in the sky?

Why wouldn't you? Probably you've been told since you were a wide-eyed child that God lives in a place called heaven, way beyond the stars. You've believed all these years that heaven is far off, and that you can't go there until you die … unless you die.

Maybe they've got great jazz up there, or great sailing. Or enough to eat and a warm, dry place to sleep, or legs you can run on. Maybe they'll put you with the right people. My friend, my wonderful old Helen, used to say in the days before she died, "As long as they put me with my husband." Surely the authorities in heaven have it all figured out, including the stumper Jesus was asked about the woman who had seven husbands. Whom would they put *her* with? Whoever *they* are.

Whatever the arrangements up there, haven't you always thought you'll only find out about God's territory after life is over? What a sad and pernicious distortion of the religious imagination.

Jesus said: *The Kingdom of God is like this: as if someone would scatter seed on the ground, and would sleep and rise night and day, and the seed would sprout and grow, he does not know how. The earth produces of itself, first the stalk, then the head, then the full grain in the head. But when the grain is ripe, at once he goes in with his sickle because the harvest has come.* (Mk. 4:26-29)

That sounds like a farm and the labour of a life and the mystery of things growing while you sleep. It sounds like the harvest is not away and gone up in the sky. In fact, you're standing in it. God's territory is in the ground under your feet.

Jesus often would say things like that. He said you can see God's place in the market and in the sea, in the bread dough rising and at a wedding. The first thing he said about God's territory is that it has come near.

Still, God's place is most often imagined as a place of pomp and grandeur, like a kind of celebrity mansion. Can you imagine God as an impertinent yellow dandelion growing up through a crack in the sidewalk? Can you see a kingdom in the bread passed from hand to hand around a table? Might it not be poor? And working? And holding hands?

If people start out with the idea that God's place is out of this world, it's little wonder they end up thinking of it seldom and caring about it less.

When Jesus told of what he called the kingdom, there was always a certain irony. For him the kingdom was not to be seen in kings or palaces. He saw a kingdom in kitchens and fields; in sweeping floors and finding lost things, lost sheep, lost children. He saw it in parties and in people lined up looking for work; in precious seeds that die in hard ground and in some that live. He saw that Solomon in all his glory was not as well turned out as any wildflower you could pick for free.

What's more, he said, God is pleased to *give* you this kingdom. Give! God is not allowing you in after you die – *if* you survive the judgment. God is not making it hard. It's free and God is happy to give it.

Let's not imagine that when Jesus tells about God's territory, he's talking about religion. Let's not imagine we won't see what he's telling about unless we die. He's telling about life. Yours. Now.

Maybe you think more about heaven than you know. Maybe heaven is about life. Hell too, for that matter.

Not many enjoy hearing Jesus tell of God's place. It can be disillusioning when heaven is brought from the sky down to earth and from the hereafter into the right now and from the triumphant glories into the humble things of an ordinary day. Who wants heaven to be here when here is, well, just here? Who wants it to be now when now is fouled by the sham and the broken dreams? One prefers a heaven that's grand.

But it's just healing and forgiving and feeding and praying and working and resting. It's just life. Is that all the Almighty has in store for us? Just life?

It may be disillusioning when first you find this out, but the one who wants to show up for heaven must learn to look down, not up. In looking down, one is looking for a patch of earth called common ground. Common ground is where Jesus is standing, telling about the harvest – the one that grows while you sleep, you're not sure how. This is God's ground, God's place. It's your place too – weeds and all.

Life will take us all there anyway, sooner or later, ready or not.

Life will take us there because aging is a great leveller. Think of W.H. Auden's observation: "into many a green valley drifts the appalling snow." He was not talking about the weather. Aging is one of the great teachers of common ground.

In the 1950s, two fabled hockey players who couldn't have been more different each wore the number 9 on his sweater. Maurice Richard grew up in the east end of Montreal, speaking French. He played for "les Canadiens." Gordie Howe grew up on a farm in Saskatchewan, speaking English. He played for the Red Wings of Detroit. They were fierce opponents on the ice.

But let the years slip away. Let it be remembered that life is lived forwards but understood backwards. What one understands after all these years is that these two players skated together in a luminous moment of the great Canadian game. They have passed together into the lore of Canadian sports because they were immensely talented at what they loved. It is not their differences that matter now, it's the common ground.

Consider this: some day your worst enemy may be the only one left who still remembers the words to Bob Dylan's The Times They Are a-Changin'.

Aging is a great leveller, but not the only one and not the only way we are led to common ground.

Were you aware that none of us is naturally profound? If we reach any profundity in life it is because life drives us down there. But here is what happens when the heart is driven down by life: it starts to widen out. The heart widens out to touch others who have been driven down by life as well. They too know pain and loss and broken dreams and seeds that fall on rocky ground.

You meet them, people you didn't have time for when you were in the illusions of your prosperity and of your longevity. You meet them, the driven down, and you see for the first time that you are sister and brother under the skin. You recognize companions – the lost and the broken and the shamed and the plain and the oppressed and the poor. You see that all along, your sisterhood and brotherhood with them was not something to be created. It had already been created. It had only to be recognized.

When at last you find yourself standing on common ground,

you have found your way into the kingdom of heaven – God's territory.

Then it begins to make sense why God gives Jesus the name that is above every other name – not because he makes it to the top, but because he makes it to the bottom.

Jesus had a way of crossing the boundaries that divide and alienate people, setting them one above the other. His way is the demand of love that takes us to common ground. One often hears people say that a church should never abandon the Bible to cross over and learn from Muslims and people of other faiths. They say a church shouldn't abandon the Bible by welcoming gays and lesbians and bisexual and transgendered people into the fullness of its life. A church shouldn't let go of the Bible in order to cross over into the territory of politics and into the struggle for clean water and refugee rights. But wait, a church doesn't do these things because it has abandoned the Bible. It does these things because it has read it.

It has seen the ground where God's odd and lowly kingdom is flourishing. The church finds life there, not by looking up to heaven, but by looking down to the place where we can stand in a sisterhood and a brotherhood of recognition.

The glorious sky heaven, if not a tarted-up impostor and an outright fraud, is at best a work-avoidance activity. Common ground is the freely given kingdom of heaven and the work of the church. When you get there you'll know yourself for the first time. You'll recognize others for the first time and you'll wonder why it took you so long to step onto ground so good.

There may be no more important text for people bedazzled by the celebrity heaven than this disillusioning and life-changing word of Jesus: . . . *the kingdom of God has come near.* . . .

Love and Marriage

I'VE BEEN MARRIED FOR 30 YEARS but I'll not put that forward as any sort of qualification. Experience is not the same thing as wisdom. Wisdom is a grandmother to the learning mind. She'll tell you it's all right to change your mind when it widens your heart.

I've changed my mind about marriage and had my mind changed by marriage many times in 30 years. It isn't over yet. I could say the same thing about 30 years of trying to interpret and articulate the wonders of sacred Scripture. I suspect that the Scripture is not so interested in fixing the mind as it is in widening the heart.

Marriage, whatever it comes to be in Canadian law and society, will not benefit from excessive sentimentality. In spite of the festivities with which it is often ushered in, marriage itself is neither a white knight nor a soaring diva. While I would be the first to encourage a joyous celebration of the marriage rite, I know that in most of its moments marriage is less like having a celebration and more like having a trade.

Marriage lays a foundation, constructs a framework and builds a house for love. Since constant perfect love is impossible (that's another story), marriage provides a structure, a habit of being together, a promise of faithfulness to carry us through those times when we know we must act with love but do not feel like loving. Eventually the house becomes a home, the wedding becomes a marriage and the relationship becomes a habit of the heart.

Marriage functions the way any good habit or discipline functions. It helps us hang on through short-term ambiguity on the way to long-term freedom. The ambiguity is in the conflict between feeling and commitment. The freedom is in knowing there's a place to stand beneath the ambiguity – common ground. Common ground is not the same as having things in common. But you find that out in time.

Because it is a habit of the heart, marriage should be hard to get out of – and into. Marriage is not casual, just as any good discipline or good house is not casually built. That's what the old tradition of an engagement is about. It's a probationary period. In most jurisdictions you can't get a licence and be married on the spot. The law requires that you afford yourself sufficient time to consider and reconsider.

Thus marriage is not a spontaneous relationship but a formal one. This is why a couple plans a wedding carefully and sets the wedding in significant traditions of people, place, apparel and language. The marriage is constituted by promises given, and its will to survive is sustained by a dependence on grace – that gift beyond explanation. Not temporary. Not casual. Not for convenience. Not as an access to rights. Not as a political positioning.

We fail to take marriage seriously when it is thought to be the private "experience" of two people. It's more than an experience. Marriage is an event that holds a couple from within and from without. The within part has to do with the love and commitment the couple generates. The without part has to do with the society's investment in marriage as a carrier of stable relationships, social cohesion and shared values.

The Christian tradition to which I belong has called marriage an "estate." In the act of marriage, two individuals leave one estate and pass into a new estate. The taking of this passage changes both of them, a transformation they enter willingly and knowingly (well, at least they know in part). They are transformed from individual artists into a collaborative work of art. This is much too perilous an undertaking for those who are concentrating on having their needs fulfilled or their rights affirmed.

Divorce, it happens. It hurts. Life must be reoriented. A way to love must be found again. The estate itself is not perfect (not to mention its occupants). Marriage is nonetheless a good house that shelters the imperfect creature's quest to persevere in love. Yet for all its good and humble powers, marriage cannot banish the sin that haunts us nor the alienation that is sin's attendant.

We bring our faith to the discussion of marriage. More importantly, it is faith that brings us. Faith brings that old question that stands at the heart of our experience as followers of Jesus; the question that runs like an aortic artery through the writings of the New Testament; the question that has haunted us from the very beginning and haunts us still: "Who is in? And who is out?"

It was this question that drove the apostle Paul to demand of the elders in Jerusalem that the Gentiles be included in the Gospel of Christ. On the road to Damascus, Paul had suddenly found himself incapacitated and then reoriented by an encounter with Christ. Paul had changed his mind. It had widened his heart.

It was this question of who was in and who was out that lay at the heart of parables like the Good Samaritan and the Prodigal Son. The same question stood in the shadows, keeping watch, as Jesus encountered a woman of a different culture at a well.

In the current discussion about same-gender marriage, these questions arise: Who will be invited to enter and live in the good house? Who will be welcome to give themselves to transformation by love in the honourable estate? Where are social values going? What is the nature of tradition? Is our morality supposed to be changing like this?

The first thing to remember about values is that value is created by God. Value is not determined by ancient custom or by current fashion or by general approval. God does not love because human creatures have value. Rather, it is in loving human creatures that God gives them value. Value is a gift – not a rule, not a partisan lever and certainly not a weapon. It is wrong to invoke the love of God so that one person's "values" might diminish another's value. Those who claim that homosexuals threaten to dismantle the value of heterosexual marriage would do well to remember that if anyone destroys marriage it is married people, not gays.

As for tradition, it is a living treasure – with emphasis on the living. Tradition is not to be confused with convention or custom or habit. These things are not themselves the light, they come to bear witness *to* the light. Convention, custom and habit are at best vessels that may hold the living tradition. This is why the Gospel of John says that the Word became a living being, not that the Word became words. The Supreme Court of Canada follows this traditional wisdom when it declares metaphorically that the Constitution is a living tree. In Christian tradition, this means that the measure by which we choose a course of action is the measure of the love of Christ, a measure that judges even the words of Scripture. It is never legitimate to use Scripture to promote a loveless agenda.

The question of morality is similar. It is important to distinguish between morals and conventions because marriage is a mystifying fabric of both these things. When we make the distinction thoughtfully, I suspect we will discover that our morals are not new at all, but our conventions have changed dramatically. The great critic Northrop Frye said that the conventions you live among will change but your morals will do you a lifetime.

In the biblical tradition there may be no more deeply "moral" issue than the Sabbath. The Sabbath is the seventh day, day of delight, doorway into the freedom and the rest of God. This is woven more deeply and more intimately into the fabric of the tradition than is marriage. The keeping of Sabbath is a commandment that requires rather than prohibits. Marriage is not required. Perhaps marriage presents itself as a profoundly moral issue because it is bound up with sexuality, and sex is bound to get our attention. Whether or not it merits so much attention is another question.

In the Gospel of Mark, Jesus says, *The Sabbath was made for humankind, and not humankind for the Sabbath.* (Mk 2:27)

If Jesus could say this of the deeply moral Sabbath, how much more might it be said of marriage? "Marriage was made for humankind, and not humankind for marriage." Said that way, the truly moral dimension of the question emerges into the light.

The question is not, "Which sexual orientations have the right to marriage?" The question is, "Who is a human being?" Who is the real, full, true human being for whom marriage is made?

Homosexuality has been variously named a disease, a crime, a sin, an aberration, a distortion, an anomaly – and those are the polite words. Like any phenomenon appearing in a minority of the population (left-handedness comes to mind), homosexuality has been subjected to a perceived need for correction. The Bible is not innocent of this anxiety nor of the bitter campaigns that arise from it. But in the living tradition, the words of the Bible are judged by the living Word to which the Bible only points. The life of the living Word is given not for correction but for redemption; not for some but for all; not as a master but as a servant.

If there is a moral issue in same-gender marriage, it is not about sex but about love. Love is judged not by its object but by its own inner qualities; that is, love's faithfulness, kindness, patience, goodness, compassion, courtesy, perseverance and sacrifice. The moral issue is our will to love one another. Beneath that moral issue lies the foundational demand to recognize the humanity of one another. The great enemy of truly moral love is not sex but fear.

In the end, moral codes, values and tradition do not decide for us. They equip us to take up the responsible and difficult task of deciding for ourselves. This deciding is itself an act of faith. So we pray for one another, we struggle to live in the love of Christ and we take our steps in humble trust that the next generation will deal generously with us, knowing we did our best with the vision of love God gave us for our day.

How then shall we be faithful to marriage? Not by forbidding change. Change is the only medium in which faithfulness can really be faithfulness. As same-gender marriage becomes part of the cultural and religious landscape of Canada, we may begin to see that our civic morality has not been cast aside. Rather, it is deepening and maturing.

All who are married and all who stand at the gate of the honourable estate deserve the hope and the prayers of those who care for them. Love is always a risk. So is life. But we believe in marriage as a good house that shelters the presence of the greatest of the gifts. It is a good house for all the people and an honourable estate from which no child of God should be turned away.

The Rising

THE MAIL HAS ARRIVED LATE TODAY, probably because of the winter rain; the sky brooding, the footing treacherous, early darkness creeping even into the chatter of the church office.

I am opening a plain brown envelope that contains about 20 pages, stapled in the upper left corner. Attached is a sticky note, beige, announcing the name of a financial management business. Underneath in blue ballpoint is a cryptic message: "This may be of interest." Beneath that, a single initial.

Printed in bold type on the cover page are six words: "Crucified, Dead and Buried: the Resurrection." I have in my hand a transcript of the CBC Radio program, *Ideas*.

I take it to my desk and, with rain pecking at the window glass, I begin to read. Soon the path through the treatise is lost. Questions have sprouted between the lines.

I am not well-acquainted with the sender. He comes to the church sometimes and listens to the distant stories of ancient Palestine, stories once scratched painstakingly on a scroll and passed hand-to-hand as generations rose and subsided. How is it that he carries these old stories of death and rising as he enters the office towers and the business lunches and the talk of level-five leadership?

"This may be of interest." Presumably it will interest me because it is my work to contemplate such things. What the note says without words is that such things have been of interest to him.

Are there many like him, going to work in one world, touched by the wonders of another? Does the commuter train bear them away in the cold air of the early morning to warm their hands at fires in the courtyards of the new Jerusalem? Does that old world still breathe strangely in them?

Yes, even now there are tales that will not die; rumours of a peasant resurrected, too insistent and too compelling to be silenced by the centuries. Thus across the millennia something causes a hand to write, "This may be of interest."

Of interest and more. The resurrection is to spiritual life as waking up is to daily life. It is how you begin, in the opening of the eyes. But when will it be more than a wistful enigma in the back of the mind? How will the resurrection appear?

Don't answer that. Don't look directly at the resurrection any more than you would look directly at the sun. You know what will happen. Besides, if you were capable of explaining it you would have so diminished the resurrection that it would no longer explain you. And you know there's no explaining you.

So I am not explaining. I don't know enough to explain. But I see that resurrection, whatever we might mean when we say the word, stirs up life out of the dust; that to find oneself in the presence of resurrection is to find oneself alive for once, as never before. I see that although it is at first fearful, before long it sends you back alive into the complexity and danger and breathtaking beauty and broken dreams of the world.

And I believe that at the heart of all this is Jesus. Jesus is the one left to us after God leaps off the high tower of heaven and takes the ghastly and gorgeous plunge down into the world, deep into the flesh. It is death to a God, resurrection, a death that works a birth in us. I can't imagine how we'd have known, if it weren't for Jesus and his dying.

IT IS NOT GIVEN TO US to look directly at the resurrection. Yet there must be a way to draw near to the fearful mystery, as Moses drew near to *the thick darkness where God was.* (Ex. 20:21) Perhaps one might go round about it, stopping here and there to look: listening now and then for strange wonders voiced by different witnesses. In the going round it may emerge somewhere, as a recluse may emerge from the trees if one does not look too directly.

Do you ever wonder – as a youth might wonder about love – if God will raise you to life at the last? He'll raise me. He'll raise me not. Which will it be, when you pull the last white petal from the bold yellow centre? God only knows. Which will it be when you put hand on rail and foot on step to climb the dark stairs? God only knows.

But look, the future tense is not the only grammar of resurrection. For us the future is not even the best tense. So let it start, this going round the fearful mystery, with the grammar of the thing.

In general, use the present tense. What might happen in the future is an endless spring of speculation. But in the end, the last word is up to God. What we may speak of intimately is the now and here. This is another way of saying (and I wish I had said it before Frederick Beuchner) that "religion is not about religion, religion is about life." If it isn't about the affairs of the day and the lump in the throat and the devastation of life by primal powers and the terrible insoluble dilemma of why there is good in the world – if it isn't about life – then it's no religion at all. Resurrection is about life, and that's why it is best cast in the present tense, as disillusioning as that might be. Ultimate futures are in someone else's hands.

And here's another point of grammar. Where possible, replace a noun with a verb. This old rule will require an immediate change in our language. What we had called "the resurrection" is better called "rising." Why speak of the resurrection when what you are confronted with is a rising? Resurrection is a concept, a theological category and a credal formula. Not that there is anything wrong with such things, but this burdened old noun desperately wants replacing by a verb. When you think of the rising and speak of it and dream of the rising and live it, you are leaving the estate of theory and crossing over into the changing landscape of happening. From the resurrection to the rising: when in the presence of a stunning happening, only a verb will do.

And from the grammar to the personality of it. The rising is shy, but not always. She is like a stranger you see across a crowded room and, like the evening itself, she is enchanted. Two disciples are walking the road to Emmaus after the crucifying. It is toward evening and the day is far spent. They find themselves talking with an enigmatic and circumspect stranger. He had not announced his coming nor does he introduce or explain himself. The rising does not appear according to any protocol or schedule. In this sense the rising can be said to be wild. That is, not domesticated. Wild does not mean irrational or chaotic. Wild will follow its own rhythms and its own voices but they are not known to us any more than the mind of the wolf or the butterfly is known. Wild things tend to be shy. So it is with the rising. Beware of any who claim to know her ways.

Nonetheless, some enchanted evening you may find yourself one of those huddled in an upstairs room, doors locked for fear, when across the crowded room you see a stranger. Uninvited. Alive. Impossible. This is to say that while she is mostly shy, there are times when the rising steps right into the upstairs room where the broken dreams are gathered. There she is! Life is on again. That's not shy, it's bold as brass.

Thank God.

The rising is not a symbol of something else, some psychology or change theory. The rising is real. Just as death is real in every life. Just as life is real in every death. The rising is not a symbol, it is a crossing over into life; life for all it's worth; life forever. Flannery O'Connor said it about the Host in the Eucharist, but I'll say it again about the rising: "Well, if it's a symbol, to hell with it." It may be a tonic to the liberal mind to understand the rising as "finding meaning in the struggle" and "the good living on after us" but we are in the presence of a power stronger, deeper and wilder than liberality. He'll think it no gift to be quoted by me, but Professor Michael Bourgeois at Emmanuel College said in a sermon to students, "the ultimately real love of God holds us in real risen life ultimately. Jesus Christ is risen indeed."

Nor will it do to confuse the rising with the splendours of the springtime. As Edna St. Vincent Millay writes: "It is not enough that yearly, down this hill, April/ Comes like an idiot, babbling and strewing flowers."

April, for all her charms, is not enough. Not enough when the issue is death and death's decadent attendant, decay. Still, Easter and springtime seem to be made for each other. The purple crocus poking its improbable little head up out of the corn snow, is that not a rising from the dead? And how can people who know Canadian winter not be gladdened by the coming of spring? Wouldn't it be odd not to delight in the power of God to awaken the cold, hard earth? Not to delight in the power of God to raise the dead?

But here's the thing: the women who first witnessed to the rising did not speak of delight. They spoke of being afraid.

Spring may come inevitably out of winter but the rising comes out of the crucifying unexpectedly and with a jolt of fear. Good Friday in all its manifestations has more power to destroy than even the longest Canadian winter. Almighty Death casts its inscrutable shadow over us, over the hospital room, over Palestine, over the reserve, over the boardroom; a shadow cast upon us as surely as sin is cast within us; darkness over the land from the sixth to the ninth hour; darkness upon the face of the deep.

If life is to emerge from this, it will not come forth inevitably as the spring emerges inevitably from the winter. There will be a mortal struggle. Almighty Death. Almighty God.

Talk of the rising is always susceptible to dangers, chief among them, sentimentality. A sentimentalist is someone who loves the good but refuses to acknowledge and to hate the evil. Sentimentality is gentle and tender and deceptive and false. To embrace the rising without knowing the dying is not only false but impossible. It is a danger to Christian truth to speak sentimentally of the rising because it disguises the terrible power of death. Disguise is the essential strategy of evil. Christians with eyes open will not celebrate Easter without having looked deeply into Good Friday.

We whom the Apostles Creed calls "the quick" have not yet seen what the rising means in all its fullness. That is because we have not yet seen what they have seen whom the Creed calls "the dead." This means that we may know the rising only in the depth and sense that we may know dying. We may know new life now only insofar as we are capable of knowing death now. In this sense Henri Nouwen wrote, "Maybe the death at the end of your life won't be so fearful if you can die well now. Yes, the real death – the passage from time into eternity, from the transient beauty of this world to the lasting beauty of the next, from darkness into light – has to be made now. And you do not have to make it alone." *

Nouwen wrote this journal passage in a terribly dispirited time, yet even then he knew it was a good time for his life to take up this word of Jesus: *The one who would save his life will lose it. The one who loses his life for my sake will find it.* (Matt. 10:39)

It's true that since we know death only in part, we know the rising only in part. But the day promised by Paul will dawn when we shall know fully even as we have been fully known. (I Cor. 13)

I HATE TO BRING IT UP HERE, the subject being such a downer and all, but there is also the matter of heresy. Heresy is something that might look like the real thing, but is definitely not. Resuscitation, or the bringing back to life of a dead person, is the heretical impersonator of the rising. Resuscitation is an impostor. It is, as historian Donald Akenson says, a literalizing and a corrupting of the rising. Tales of "shrouds and revivified corpses" were told, it is true. But if we take them to mean either resuscitation or resurrection, we have lost touch with the power of the rising.

It is not about getting back what once you were. It is about being transformed by the hand of God. That's why it costs everything. That's why it leads not to winning, which is the way to keep all you were and add on some extra glories. The rising leads to victory, which is the way to lose all you were and be transformed into something God alone can see.

Death ends a life, but not a relationship. The rising continues to happen. Here shy, there bold, always wild, the rising appears now and again because after all, God has taken the plunge. And the taking of it has riddled the earth with heaven. The taking of it has impregnated death with life. The last thing the church should do is to shut down that plunging presence by freezing it in the Scripture and worshipping it in the text and mistaking it for the impostor called resuscitation. The rising is not the stunning accomplishment of an individual but the rebirth of a relationship across a terrible divide. Jesus always appears to people, with people, for people – never as a solitary demonstration of personal aggrandizement.

The witness of the sacred texts does not speak of the risen Christ in isolation. So whatever this is, it cannot be all about you personally. It's not even all about Jesus. The rising is all about relationship. We look for its wild and shy presence not in the mirror of the mind but in the faces of others.

It seems to come with strangers, or at least with those not at first recognized as friends. It seems to come at table where food and drink are given. In the midst of such sharing of life's sustenance, the living presence appears inexplicably.

It seems to come when the *I am who I will be*, the inscrutable God of justice, is honoured, loved and obeyed in the ordinary things of the day. It is a humble thing, really; and in the midst of the day's great bombastic sounds it is the little song of grace that opens the heart to life in Jesus Christ.

If you want to see the rising, look into the face of the stranger who falls in beside you on the road. Listen to the voice telling you of God's stunning hope in spite of all the evidence. Invite the stranger in. Share what you have. Oh yes, and go to church to hear the text, the tradition and the community bear witness to this irrepressible life by the grace and strength of God.

When God comes down from the sky, coming as a bird would fly over a river, there is an awakening and a giving of one's life. Everything is more real. There is the hearing of a different voice. This is it. Life. Full. All of it. Now. So laugh, work, dance, love, share, enjoy, do justice, love kindness, walk humbly. Stare death in the face. Watch God die. Weep. But at the end of it all, don't close your eyes. The best is yet to be.

We have been raised to life with Christ. Paul said this interesting thing about the rising. He said, We have been raised. He didn't say that you might be raised if you're good, or lucky. He didn't say you will be raised someday when it's time to go to heaven. He speaks of your life now. You have been raised to life with Christ.

TROUBLE IS, IT MAKES A TERRIBLE DIFFERENCE if you don't know that you've been raised to life with Christ; if you are unaware of what God has given you; if it hasn't dawned on you that to hear the Easter news of the risen Christ is to hear Easter news about yourself; if you don't know that God who gives life to Christ gives life to you and that it's one life indivisible, to which you both belong. If you don't realize such things then you are likely to choose the sort of life that we have become all too familiar with over the years.

Really, God must look with bewilderment, when having so clearly and powerfully opened the door for us, we head directly for the same old prisons; the old familiar tombs; ignoring the fearful light of Easter to crawl into the safer gloom behind the stone. We choose this because this is the life we know. We've grown accustomed to its face. It is no surprise, after all, that the first emotion of the rising is fear. Fear of living. Fear of living without a net. Fear of life in a different world, God's world, where even the stones cry out. It is the choice of every life to hear in the words of Paul an invitation, or a sentence: *You have been raised to life with Christ.*

She'll raise me, she'll raise me not: the delicate white petals are detached so easily from the bold yellow centre.

DON'T LOOK BACK. This injunction has a certain wisdom at times, but it is not a universal law. In many places the Bible demands that we look back in order to remember the former things and to dig once more the ancient wells. But sometimes looking back turns you into a pillar of salt. (Gen. 19) The salt episode is a good one to remember in the presence of the rising. Looking back to capture the rising as if it were lodged in the past is as deadly to its truth as capturing a living creature in a sealed bottle. This is why the Gospel says, *You are looking for Jesus. He is not here. He has risen. He has gone ahead of you. Go, you will find him.* (Matt. 28:5-7)

Practice

A Genealogy of Transformation

THERE ARE THINGS one never manages to accomplish in life:

- You can't turn back the clock.
- You can't make somebody love you.
- You can't take back a word once it is spoken.
- You can't see the face of God.
- You can't live forever.
- You can't take it with you.

Disappointing as it is, life is surrounded by limits. Not only surrounded, life is inhabited by limits. At first they appear to diminish life, to hem it in and render it frail. In many ways this is true. It is often the case that the spirit is willing but the flesh is weak.

Yet recognizing these limits does not diminish life nor must it lead to resignation and despair. Acknowledging the boundaries within which we live actually does something quite the opposite. It leads to the recognition that life is precious. Time is precious because it is not limitless; love is too, because it cannot be purchased. True friends are precious because they are few. Words are precious because once you say them you cannot get them back again.

If you have a limited supply of things, each one is of great value. In the Daniel Defoe novel, Robinson Crusoe is shipwrecked and marooned alone. Seeing his foundered ship a few hundred yards from shore, he fashions a raft and makes 11 trips to the wreck in order to salvage what he can. After each trip he makes a careful list of the items he has saved from the sea. Each thing is meticulously noted because it is so precious.

If you have an endless supply of things, none of it is precious. Things can be used up, discarded, replaced. What that says for consumer culture is startling. Often North Americans are accused of loving their possessions too much because they are always buying and replacing, buying and replacing. But consumer culture doesn't teach you to love possessions, it teaches you to despise them. The problem is not that things are worth too much to us; the problem is they are worth too little. Why? Because there are no limits. And where there is no awareness of limits, there is no sense of the precious, no wonder, no gratitude.

When life teaches you its limits – that life is short, that deep friendships are few, the human creature frail in the great sweep of cosmic history – then life itself begins to appear as a miracle. Less is more. Wonder is born.

One simple exercise of the spiritual life is to take a meditative walk of thanksgiving. The purpose of such a walk is to notice something along the way. It may be something seen in a physical sense. It may be a memory that wants noticing or a face that appears before the eyes of the soul. Whatever or whoever it is, wonder is what happens when you really notice. In this sense, wonder is a sister to prayer, prayer being the art of paying attention. When wonder has opened a crack to let light in, gratitude follows quickly to widen the heart with a natural and spontaneous thankfulness. Thus, wonder is the first movement and gratitude the next.

One summer I visited the people of a little village on the shore of the North Thompson River in the interior of British Columbia. They had found themselves in the path of a Category 6 wildfire. When the fire came there was nothing for them to do but run away.

A Category 6 wildfire is a fire of such magnitude that it consumes not only its primary fuel – the trees – but it reaches up to consume huge volumes of oxygen in the air. It becomes a fireball in the sky, creating winds with the power of a hurricane and bellowing with the scream of a jet engine. The fire burns beneath the ground as well, eating through root systems and burning up through trees from the bottom. Unnoticed until the sap is superheated, the trees suddenly explode, sending shards of burning wood high into the sky.

When you've been in the presence of a Category 6 wildfire you have witnessed one of the primal powers of the earth. You are on intimate terms with the frailty of the human creature, and if you survive, even if everything you own has been destroyed, you are – surprisingly enough – grateful.

When I visited the people in the village the first thing I noticed among them was their gratitude. Any bravado or arrogance that may have existed among them seemed to have slipped away. Every person, from child to grandparent, knew that a great and terrible power had drawn near to them. They knew what it meant to be saved.

Even though there was nothing but a charred place on the ground where a home had once stood, there was gratitude. Even though they stood before a monumental task of rebuilding, they were grateful to be alive, because it might have been otherwise. I could not keep track of the number of times I heard homeless and jobless people say, "Thank God."

Gratitude is the prelude to happiness. It is very difficult to be grateful and unhappy at the same time. There was a happiness in the community one does not encounter in the richest gated compound in the country. They shared the tasks of feeding, clothing and sheltering one another in ways they had never experienced before. This community showed that even in the most difficult circumstances, gratitude is not beyond reach. When gratitude is present, happiness is never far away, although happiness is shy and does not like to be looked at. This is why the French say that happiness is written in white ink. You can't grasp happiness or buy it or preserve it. It's sort of like manna. But gratitude is its test. When you practice gratitude, happiness will appear.

My friend Florence comes to mind. Florence was an imp of a woman; a grandmother, an eccentric and a purveyor of not a little mischief. She had been orphaned as a small child and all her life she was grateful for her own children and happy in belonging to her family.

Florence was grateful for books. She was happy to volunteer in the library, introducing children to the delight of reading. She was happy in her garden, grateful for the sun and for the rain. She was happy at the sound of children skipping rope on the sidewalk. I remember speaking with her just a few days before she died. She had cancer and we both knew perfectly well the end was near. She said to me:

"What a wonderful way to die. All my senses remind me of the great gifts I have been given in my life. I am overwhelmed by the feeling that I am on my way to some place that is perfect in every dimension. And if not, I know I'll be having a good long sleep."

Happiness blossoms in generosity. Florence lived a generous life in the presence of the kind of hardship and pain that might have borne bitter fruit. But it didn't. It was gratitude that nurtured her happiness and her generous character.

Here's something to know about character: it can never be possessed, only enacted. Character is not something you have like you might have brown eyes or an introverted personality. Character is like faith, it is something you enact. It does not exist until you act it into life. To say that Florence *had* a generous character would not be quite the right way to describe it. She *practised* a generous character. She *enacted* it. She is one of my heroes.

Heroes are important mentors as we learn character. There are heroes for sport, heroes for politics, for art and for war. But in the alternative world of the Christian life, heroes are people who give, people who serve and who practise a character deepened by self-sacrifice.

I remember Anne speaking in our church one day about this. She told about how she had learned the generous character from her father; how he would come home at the end of the week and set out the week's pay according to the family's needs. But always, first, there was something given – something for the church or for charity or for someone else. This was done in the presence of the whole family, adults and children alike. All were learning and practising the generous character.

Perhaps some of us began to learn this from parents or grandparents when we were small too. Maybe we got a small allowance every week or maybe we earned little bits of money by helping out. We were taught to set aside a few pennies for charity or in some other way for the work of God.

And notice this: they taught us first to set aside something to be given. They did not say, "See if you have something left over at the end of the week and if there is something, you can give it." They wanted us to learn the generous character not by chance but by choice. They wanted giving to be a first thought, not an afterthought.

It is clear in retrospect that the few pennies were not about the financing of institutions. What the parent or grandparent was teaching was not finance but the way of a generous character.

Like the mustard seed that grows and is transformed into shelter for many, generosity transforms lives. Yes, it is counterintuitive. It seems it ought to be more blessed to receive than to give. But somehow we know that life was not made to be that way. We are happier in generosity than in acquisitiveness. Life is abundant when lived in a generous spirit. We know this because we've known people who have followed the path to a generous life. It is a good place to end up and is open to all who choose to live there.

So, in this life there is a genealogy of transformation. It is something like this:

- The recognition of limits is the prelude to wonder.
- Wonder is pursued by gratitude.
- Gratitude is the test of happiness.
- Happiness opens to generosity.
- Generosity transforms lives.

Gin and Grape Juice

THE CONGREGATION I BELONG TO began life in 1791 as the Fredericton Methodist Church. It had 13 members and met in the home of a man named Duncan Blair. We had a rough start.

No sooner had we held our first meeting than the Anglicans had our minister arrested and charged before the court with spreading false doctrine. Happily, the Governor decided in our favour and we survived. We've long since forgiven the Anglicans.

The life of any congregation is much too deep and rich to be lived in the one dimension of the present: as if we had neither the blood of forebears nor the mythology of ancestors haunting our psyche; as if the tomorrows of our children were of no great significance, and we had nothing but the present to care about or live for. There isn't enough air in the present for a church to breathe.

G.K. Chesterton said: "Tradition may be defined as an extension of the franchise. Tradition means giving votes to the most obscure of all classes, our ancestors. It is the democracy of the dead. Tradition refuses to submit to the small and arrogant oligarchy of those who merely happen to be walking about." (*Prophet of Orthodoxy*)

My congregation is Methodist by tradition. We were born in the year John Wesley died.

The long life of the founder of Methodism spanned the 18th

century in England. In order to catch a glimpse of Wesley's England it might not be a bad idea to start with a recipe. A recipe for a medicine that became wildly popular in the London of the 1700s consisted of fermented corn, juniper berries, root of angelica, orris and coriander seeds. Gin.

It was invented in Holland as a medicine thought to cure digestive problems, gout and the pain of gallstones. It was brought to England by soldiers who called it Dutch Courage. It caught on quickly.

In the first half of the 18th century, England's consumption of gin increased from 680,000 gallons per year to 11 million. William of Orange had ended trade with France so wine and brandy were not available. Gin flourished. It was made and sold so widely that it supplanted the common drink of weak beer. Nobody in their right mind in London drank the water.

By 1750, gin was being manufactured and sold in every fourth household in London. Grocers made it; so did weavers, chandlers, pedlars, hawkers, barbers, tobacconists. Gin was fed to babies to placate them. The city went on a colossal bender.

The effect of the wildly popular new medicine on London's poor was devastating. Labourers drank gin supplied on credit against their wages. The result was poverty, theft, disease and the poorhouses filled with human misery. The infant mortality rate was 75 percent. London's population went into decline as the death rate exceeded surviving births. This was the era of the Hogarth prints such as the famous "Gin Lane" which depicts a chaotic London laneway with children falling out of the arms of drunken mothers, people fighting dogs for scraps and bones, and the dead being hauled through the streets in wheelbarrows. Misery, poverty, sickness, degradation and death reign in Gin Lane.

This is the London of John Wesley. This is where Methodism was born. Wesley saw the effects on the people. He knew that the government did not concern itself with the poor. The care of the poor was the responsibility of the parishes. He saw the government relying on tax income from the sale of gin and called it a "commerce in human life." He said that the government was selling the flesh and blood of their countrymen. "And why is food so dear?" he asked. "The grand cause is because such immense quantities of corn are continually consumed in distilling."

On humanitarian grounds, Wesley pleaded for an end to the gin trade. As odd as it might seem, neither Wesley nor the early Methodists were teetotallers. Beer was served in early Methodist reading rooms. Wesley was not involved in a moral campaign against alcohol as much as he was involved in a political, economic and humanitarian campaign against a government that took profit from human misery. Later, Wesley's followers would become more Wesleyan than he was and reduce his struggle to a caricature by concentrating on the moral evil of alcohol and the moral virtue of abstinence.

Through the efforts of the Methodists and others who engaged in the political struggle to end the gin trade, the government eventually took action. At first it tried to license retailers but that just put reputable shopkeepers out of business and encouraged the black market. Eventually the government succeeded in separating the manufacture of gin from its sale. Manufacturers could not sell on the street. Vendors could not manufacture. That separation of manufacture and sale, along with the licensing of both, is why even today if you want to buy a bottle of the Dutch Courage, you have to go to the government-approved liquor store. That is Methodist history alive and well in Canada.

Knowing this part of our story, one is not surprised that in our congregation we use grape juice in the communion service. We do it as a witness to the cup of human suffering. We do it as a way of remembering the struggles of our ancestors and the courage with which they faced the social destruction of their day. It was in this context that the Methodists also became founders in public education, credit unions and the labour movement.

It is surprising and not a little disheartening to hear people of the Methodist tradition saying that the church should not be involved in politics or in economics or in trade or in government or in the social issues of the day. It is stunning to hear people who have John Wesley for an ancestor say the church should stick to religion as if religion had nothing to do with the gin lanes and the shelters and the boardrooms and the legislatures of our time. These would be the same people who think we drink the cup of suffering and salvation in grape juice as a matter of personal piety. That would be to trivialize and eviscerate a more complex, terrible and courageous truth. We drink the Lord's cup in grape juice because we remember the suffering and we are committed to work in the streets and in the halls of government for the people who suffer today, the beloved of God.

In this way we remember that religion is not about religion – it's about life.

John Wesley was still alive when the congregation I belong to held its first service. In 1791, the village of Fredericton had 500 inhabitants and 15 taverns.

Gin has gone through many mutations in the streets of our city. Now it goes by names like ecstasy and cocaine. Still we are summoned to the struggle our ancestors knew.

Wesley is gone. The great Methodist preacher George Whitefield is gone. The hymnwriter Charles Wesley, the courageous campaigner Nellie McClung, the visionary J.S. Woodsworth – all gone. There is nobody here but us chickens to see this implicated Gospel alive today. The church is many generations old but it's only one generation deep.

So we will do in our time what they did in theirs until that day we taste the new wine at the table in the commonwealth of God. Until then, I'm happy with communion in grape juice. We were Methodist, you know.

Land of Love and Anger

In 2004, Peter Short was part of a nine-member delegation of Canadian church leaders and officials who travelled to the Middle East to witness and support Israelis and Palestinians working for peace.

EVERY LIFE IS A WITNESS TO SOMETHING or to someone. Whether or not it is clear to us, every life is a proclamation, a testimony to some great dream or to some implacable desolation or both. Our lives can be many things but they cannot be neutral. To say it another way: you may be able to avoid making up your mind but you can't avoid making up your life.

All this is brought to my mind in Beirut as I listen to Armenian Patriarch Aram the First speaking to our delegation. His Holiness fixes us with blazing eyes, his speaking punctuated by great peals of laughter. But he is clear and serious as he tells us: "We have to get along with our identities. I have a certain distaste for the word 'presence.' We Christians are a small minority but we are not just a presence. Our great challenge is to maintain a witness and an engagement, not against others, but for the reconciling love of God in Jesus Christ. We face the challenge of how to be fully ourselves without being against someone else."

Conviviality is a word often on his lips. It means living

together, an urgent and obvious necessity in Lebanon. But the call to conviviality is not to be interpreted as a call to extinguish identity.

Every life is a witness and every Christian life is a witness to the redeeming and reconciling love of God in Jesus Christ. This witness is the vocation of every Christian community whether in Barrie or Beirut, Jerusalem or Jonquière.

I learn a lot about Canada by going to the Middle East. Visiting people who belong to the small but ancient Arab Christian minorities in Lebanon, Syria, Israel and Palestine helps me to see the cost of witness at home in places where Christians are a small minority, places like the Lower Mainland of British Columbia, the most secular area in the country.

In the Middle East, much is devastating and much is inspiring. I am humbled before the inscrutable mystery of it: how the intractable problems of this land can be held in place by so much love and by so much anger. I don't understand – nobody understands. There is no objective vantage point from which to assess the 10,000 ancient and contemporary strands that weave the coat of many colours in which this land and its peoples are clothed.

The hills and the sky are dreadfully beautiful. The killing is just dreadful. Every faction has a genuine grievance, every leader expresses hope for peace. No sooner is one assessment put forward than its alternative, if not its opposite, is waiting for a hearing. I can't make up my mind. Much better minds and deeper hearts than mine have been struggling here since time immemorial. But here's the thing – I may not be able to make up my mind but I know that the long labour of the Middle East conflict is bearing children in Canada. I've seen it in the Concordia University riots, in the racial profiling of Arabs and in anti-Semitic attacks on sacred places. I learn a lot about Canada by being in Israel and Palestine. It is clear to me as never before that it is in Canada that I must make up my life.

Take the Israeli settlements in Palestine, for example. They begin with trailers on hilltops. In a few short months there are homes. The military arrives to provide protection. Before long there is urban infrastructure, perimeter clearing, private settlement roads cutting through and dividing up Palestinian lands.

When a Palestinian scientist calls these settlements colonies, something moves in my mind. Who are we Canadians to criticize Israelis? We wrote the book on colonies. We've built great cities and vast farms on confiscated land and confined the former inhabitants to designated areas. We call them reserves. I recognize the anger in the Middle East because I see it at home.

I learn something else from Naim Ateek, a Palestinian Christian and a new friend. He is the director of Sabeel, a centre for liberation theology in Jerusalem. I learn from Naim that the Arabic verb *shaheda* means to witness and that a *shahid* is a martyr. I already know that the English word for witness comes from the Greek *martus* which means one whose life is given as a testimony to something or to someone. Soon after we arrive in Jerusalem I will learn that such words are another strand in the coat of many colours.

It is Sunday, the spring sunshine bathing the streets of Jerusalem, when we learn a young man named George Khoury has been murdered in a drive-by shooting while jogging in the streets. He was 20 years old, a Christian Arab, graduate of the Anglican International School in Jerusalem, a student at the Hebrew University, the middle son of Elias Khoury, a lawyer well-known for his work in the struggle against the confiscation of Palestinian lands for Israeli settlements.

The murderers belong to the Al-Aksa Martyrs Brigade. Their organization issues a statement saying the killing is a case of "mistaken identity." They thought the young man was a settler. George was hit twice in the head, once in the neck and once in the stomach. A neighbourhood resident who heard the shots ran to his side. He tried to stop the bleeding from the head wound. He said that George tried to say something but he couldn't.

Many at Sabeel know George and his family. His father has

been a valued member of the centre's board. The news shocks and saddens everyone we meet. For us it is a particularly moving scene in a drama already becoming too familiar. On the first day of our visit, six people are killed in Gaza. On the second, there are seven killings. On the third it is young George. The next morning we awaken to the ominous news that Sheikh Yassin of Hamas has been assassinated along with his son and six associates.

The threats of retaliatory killing hover in the air of the Jerusalem morning. The city is on full alert. From loudspeakers the mosques broadcast haunting musical laments over the city. Everywhere there are young soldiers – teenaged men and women – with assault rifles at the ready. I know the fear of Israelis in every bus that stops beside us. I taste the bitter anxiety in the back of the throat.

I know this fear but not as viscerally as it is known by Israelis who inhabit this land in memory of the Holocaust and in the promise that never again will there be a world where there is no safe place for Jews to come home to.

And I know this anger but not as viscerally as it is known by Palestinians who pay the price of generations in refugee camps and who are not citizens of any country on earth.

The Israelis are making sure the past does not return. The Palestinians are desperately trying to bring it back.

Meanwhile, we are making up our lives in Canada, the beloved and troubled country. Here I am learning more deeply the truth of St. Augustine's warning: "Never condemn evil as if it were something that arose entirely outside of yourself." We must give every encouragement to Canadian politicians and diplomats who work toward a peaceable, just, negotiated settlement – not only for colonies on the other side of the world but for our own. We must join and support groups of people – Jewish and Muslim, Aboriginal and Christian – who take the risk of conviviality. We must contribute to the witness and the work of this United Church of ours, the work of finding common ground and a place at the table for all. We must pray for the peace of Jerusalem and for strength to walk the reconciling way of Jesus Christ.

At the funeral for George Khoury, someone reads a message from Al Aksa saying that from the point of view of the organization, George was a *shahid* (martyr, witness). The congregation shouts, "No! No!" They refuse to let his life be co-opted and labelled in this way. Something in them knows that he was a talented and beloved young man, full of the promise of his rich heritage and his bright future. Something in them knows that he is a witness not to terror but to what, with God's help, we yet might be: a young life running in the sunshine.

Coming Home to Africa

*In 2005, Peter Short went to Angola, where the United Church has been
active and welcomed for many years. He was accompanied by his spouse,
Sue, an educator, and Gary Kenny, the United Church's staffperson for
Southern Africa.*

IT'S 8 A.M. ON OUR FIRST DAY IN AFRICA and already 35 degrees.
We are driving through Luanda, Angola's capital city of three million.
The streets are broken, littered, choked with cars and people.

Before long we are standing in the blinding sun outside a
Congregational church. A choir in dark blue gowns and white yokes
is waiting to enter the small cinder block building with empty windows and corrugated steel roof. Inside where it's dark, 655 people are
packed onto low benches. Some, unable to get in, are standing outside at the windows.

This congregation worships in Umbundu and Portuguese.
The service begins with a hymn. I can't decipher the words but I
recognize a tune I know from home, It Is Well With My Soul. This
odd companionship between the strange and the familiar will be a
constant and haunting refrain in the days ahead.

Two hours later I'm drenched with sweat, shaking 655 hands
as people emerge from the church. We are bowing and saying *"Bom*

Dia!" in our feeble Portuguese. The worship, led by a bright young woman in clerical collar, has blended a certain formality with wonderful dancing and music led by keyboard, bass and guitar.

I am impressed by the vitality of the congregation and greatly relieved that the task of preaching for the first time in Africa is behind me. (I had been wondering if they'd be mystified and disappointed by my pale North American version of the Gospel of Christ.) I marvel that so many people come to this place, dressed in their best, cheerful and hospitable in the heat.

WE ARE DRIVING ONCE MORE, this time through a *musseque*, on our way to the second service of the morning. The polite term for a *musseque* is "informal settlement." As far as the eye can see, people are living in patched-together shelters without electricity or running water. Most of these dwellings are made of mud brick or salvaged sheets of corrugated steel, their roofs secured by the weight of large stones.

Hundreds of thousands of people have left their homes in the rural areas, seeking safety from the wars that have destroyed this country for a generation. Their fields back home are sown with landmines; tanks have torn up the immensely beautiful countryside.

Here they exist under sheets of metal, the air shimmering in thick heat. In Canada we may have no word for *musseque*, but there are places I remember, places on First Nations reserves and in the backside of towns. We may not have the words, but we recognize the tune.

From 1961 to 2002, Angola endured one long devastating war. At one point Cuban soldiers were defending oil installations owned by Americans against Angolan insurgents who were equipped and supported by South Africa and the United States. Angola became an international battlefield of the Cold War.

Today it is in a state of complex emergency. A fragile peace stands between the people and the spectre of recurring war. The challenges of healing and rebuilding are beyond imagination. Honorary Canadian Consul Allan Cain says that the government, for all its corruption and imperfection, needs encouragement in its efforts to clear landmines, resettle ex-combatants and develop civil infrastructure. Critique may be essential to democracy; but in this complex emergency, critique with the power to destabilize can lead to war. Here the church must decide whether its public witness is to contribute to compromise or to make the church feel righteous about itself.

We are driving through the *musseque* over garbage packed down like pavement between the mud holes. Everywhere people are selling things – coat hangers, cans of gas, windshield wipers, vegetables, garbage bags, cans of Fanta. They stand in the traffic, they sit under tarps beside the road. This is called the informal economy. To my eye it looks chaotic but Gary Kenny, who has been here before, says it is only chaotic to the untutored eye.

But now we are arriving at the Jericho Parish, cinder block walls, steel roof, dirt floor, low benches. Like the last church, this one is full of people and overwhelming heat. How do they do this?

The pastor, Andre Cangoui, welcomes us. His English is excellent but he is speaking to his congregation in Portuguese. Augusto Chipesse tells me, "He is inviting you to preach. He acknowledges that you are not scheduled to do this but he is saying that surely the people would be happy to hear the guest from Canada."

I say, "Of course." But it's not exactly what I am thinking.

"*Irmaos em Cristo, Bom dia!*" (My knowledge of Portuguese is exhausted in this one simple greeting.) I am standing behind the pulpit; it's dressed for the occasion in white satin and purple ribbon. There are hundreds and hundreds of expectant faces before me. Once again I am struck by the touching of the alien and the familiar. Outside is the sprawling daily struggle for survival. In here is the power of Joshua and the ancient story of hope in God. I begin the unexpected sermon (Augusto translating):

"In Canada we sometimes hear the phrase 'Mother Africa.' Have you heard this phrase?" There is general nodding and sounds of approval. Angolan congregations encourage the preacher with murmurs of affirmation.

"To say 'Mother Africa' is to acknowledge that in its primal origins the human creature was born in Africa. No matter where we come from or where we get to in the earth, Africa is where our human journey began. In some ancient way, beneath our understanding yet common to us all, everybody comes from Africa. Therefore, whoever comes to Africa is coming home. Thank you for welcoming me home."

Even as I speak I know that the words are right and that I do not understand them. "Whoever comes to Africa is coming home." In these words, the alien and the familiar stare intently at one another, as if searching for a glimmer of recognition. There is no resolution, not yet. It is impossible just now to reconcile the musseque with any notion I have of home.

I will spend the rest of the visit, and the months and years ahead, trying to recognize home in the unfamiliar faces, unknown languages and cityscapes. I become aware that this recognition of which I am not yet capable is what Jesus did. Somehow, in his healing and feeding, his living and dying, and in his rising, he opened the gate and led us out of our alien places. He brought us home to the common ground of our humanity – home, if you will, to Mother Africa.

IN THE AFTERNOON we go to a meeting of about 50 pastors and leaders of the Congregational Church. I ask, "Why do people come and fill up the churches?" A man stands to respond, "We come because of the suffering. We know that the only comfort we have is in the church."

Another adds: "Our communal way of life has been destroyed, overpowered by colonial culture. We try to recover that life as best we can in our church."

I ask, "What is the greatest challenge you face?" A young pastor responds that it is "the redeeming of the spirit of the Angolan man from dependency and violence so that we can see one another as human beings again."

I recognize in his words a heart-stopping task, requiring courage and the hope that is a gift of the Spirit. I am grateful for the encouragement I receive from this young man who dreams like God.

At this meeting I first hear the name Kirkwood, a name I will hear many times in the coming days (pronounced in Angola as if it had no "w"). Luciano Chianeque, the pastor of the church where we are gathered, tells how Rev. Jim Kirkwood, the United Church's longtime secretary for Southern Africa, now retired, recognized something in him and helped him pursue his education in South Africa.

Over the following days I will hear other names: Burgess, Snow, Radley, Bridgman. Ricardo Ulianeque, the former general secretary of the Council of Churches, asks us to thank them and to pray for them. "They formed us," he said. "If it were not for them we would have disappeared. Pray that the work of your grandparents not be lost."

This plea would become a refrain. The church in Angola remembers the times before the civil war. Now that the war is over they wonder why the mission stations cannot be reopened, with their gardens, clinics and schools. They ask, "Why don't you return and live with us again?"

I know the answers: our mission philosophy has changed, indigenous capacity must be encouraged, government must be lobbied to be responsive to the needs of the people, partnerships have replaced patronizing aid, the old way abetted imperialism. But when they ask, the answers turn feeble in my mouth.

Now here, gathered with the pastors, one woman asks if female pastors in Canada can work full-time for the church or if they must have other jobs as well. Another asks Sue to speak, and Sue tells of her experience as a mother and her work in the church. The women are so delighted with her presence that they decide to name a new, uncompleted women's centre after her. It is located on the grounds of a school run by the church and supported by the Mission and Service Fund. Later, Sue would lay a concrete block in the foundation, and a small ceremony would recognize the connection between women of Angola and women of Canada. I see again the linked spirituality of women, and I know that Sue lives closer to Mother Africa than I do.

A FEW DAYS LATER we drive from Huambo, a city in the central highlands, to Dondi, a mission station financed, built and staffed by The United Church of Christ (Congregational) and The United Church of Canada. The drive is only 60 km but it takes two hours. Beside the road we see the red-and-white painted stones that warn of areas laced with landmines. The countryside is beautiful beyond description. And deadly.

I knew Dondi had once been a thriving mission station; but I was not prepared for the fact it had been a small town. There had been a hospital, schools, a seminary and residences. There had been a small church and then a much larger one, both standing roofless and forlorn as the forest reasserts its relentless dominion. There had been workshops and barns. A river runs through it and the eye is drawn to the hills, green in the distance. The mission consists of 3,400 hectares of the loveliest land you could ever want to see.

The local Congregational church was trying to run a school in one of the abandoned buildings but the government had closed it because of inadequate sanitary and safety conditions. No roof, for example. The church is now making repairs, hoping to reopen the school.

The local pastor doesn't say it but I know he wonders if we will be able to help. The people of his congregation, who have come to sing for us, are hoping too. So am I, but I'm not sure what to hope for. I know that Mission and Service Fund dollars go in a block grant to the Evangelical Congregational Church in Angola (IECA), which is funding this project. I know IECA's resources are stretched thin and that we don't intervene in the priorities of our partners. But the old mission and the new are at war in my mind. Couldn't we find a way to get good people in Canada involved in building this school?

From Dondi we go on to Lobito. In all of Angola today, we have only one "overseas personnel," Margaret Edwards, a marvellous person from Qualicum Beach on Vancouver Island, who belongs to Parksville United Church. She teaches in the Canata Educational Centre in Lobito, which is also supported by our gifts to the Mission and Service Fund. We visit Margaret, delivering the duct tape she has requested from Canada.

In Lobito the next day, in an outdoor amphitheatre filled with 700 people, I preach about the power in the name of Jesus. With my new friend and mentor Jose Chipenda translating, I remind the people of Paul's assertion that God has given Jesus the name that is above every other name, above all the celebrity names, above the mountains and beyond the stars.

I am aware as I speak that the name above all others is a Christian claim that grates on all who are sensitive to the cultural imperialism in which our Gospel has been dressed, a wolf in lamb's clothing. I am aware that guilt about Christian disregard for indigenous spiritualities and Christian complicity in the destruction of indigenous cultures has rendered many of us silent about the name of Jesus.

But I speak this way just the same – not because I want to ignore the responsibility we carry – but because Paul was not talking about Jesus making it to the top. Paul says that Jesus received the name above every other name because in his humble obedience to God's way, he made it to the bottom of human experience. He made it down into the place of hunger where he broke bread. He made it down to the place of sin where he offered forgiveness. He took into himself suffering, shame and godforsakenness. He entered the place of death. He brought God's ultimate companionship to our frailty. He showed us our God-given human unity, a unity we don't have to create, only to recognize. One could say he took us home to our common ground, Mother Africa.

THIS IS THE PLACE I am seeking in the bullet-riddled buildings of Huambo, in the eyes of the boy selling onions by the road and in the strange-sounding songs sung in Umbundu to a tune from Victorian England. I see this human quest written long ago in the language of the Epistle to the Hebrews: *They confessed that they were strangers and foreigners on the earth, for people who speak in this way make it clear that they are seeking a homeland. If they had been thinking of the land they had left behind, they would have had opportunity to return. But as it is, they desire a better country, that is, a heavenly one. Therefore God is not ashamed to be called their God; indeed, he has prepared a city for them.* (Hebrews 11:13f)

Back in Canada now, I know more deeply what it is to be a stranger and a foreigner. I think I have understood something of what it means to be seeking a homeland. I know that the better country is not behind but ahead. The better country is not in a nation but in a humanity. The better country is not in a strategy but in a Christ.

To Christ belongs the victory from the depths of our humanity. His victory will never belong to us, but we must belong to his victory if ever we are to make it home. May God grant us the heart to see the city prepared and the faith to walk together toward its lights.

Prophecy

Wild Roses

MUCH IN THE SPIRITUAL TRADITION falls into the realm of the unlikely, because the spiritual tradition has its face turned toward the living and radiant one. The eyes struggle to see but from the human point of view, God is so unlikely, so stunning, sometimes so unsightly and always so impossible. And this is the way it must be. Or God would not be God at all.

Jonah comes to mind. That Jonah got swallowed and lived in the belly of a great fish until he got spit out alive on the beach – not likely.

That the waters of the Red Sea drew back to permit the Israelites to cross over – not likely.

That Jesus was born of a virgin. Well, you know what Karl Barth said about that: the great theologian said the virgin birth is a doctrine posted on guard at the gate of the mystery of Christmas. No one should think they can hurry past this sentry, reminding all who enter this region that they set their feet upon a road at their own cost and risk. The virgin birth is a warning against walking blithely amongst the demands and dangers of the Gospel. Faith will demand reason all right, but it will demand something deeper than calculation and higher than mental capacity. It is this greater requirement of faith that causes the spiritual tradition to fall so often into the realm of the unlikely.

That Jesus was raised from the dead – not likely.

As unlikely you might say as a rose growing red and fragrant in the cold wind of winter. A book title comes to mind: W.O. Mitchell's *Roses Are Difficult Here*.

And so they are. Roses are difficult in the Canadian climate in which Mitchell writes and in which we live, every bit as difficult as lives of kindness and courage and grace are difficult where you live.

Suppose you had to choose a title for your life and your work. Suppose you had to say in a phrase what it's like to be inside your skin and to live the struggle you live. Don't you think that might be a good title? Roses Are Difficult Here.

In my work, day after day I receive stories that would break your heart. People under stress. People alone, lonely and afraid. People starving for encouragement. People thirsty for a word from the Lord, even in the church where the Lord is a mantra and a motto. People whose lives and work have become a bitter day in December. Roses! Difficult? People are all the time telling me that roses are impossible here.

But here's the thing. It's not problems that steal the life out of you. In fact, when you think about it, you've no doubt overcome many obstacles in your life. It's not stress that turns out the lights in the interior castle. Some of your great and shining moments have happened in the most stressful circumstances.

It's not the presence of problems or the presence of stress that makes roses difficult here. It's not the presence of anything. It's an absence. It's an abandoned and boarded-up heaven. It's the silence of God and the aloneness in facing the world that makes roses so unlikely.

At the same time we know that the absence, for all its dread, is not new. Our people have seen this before. It is recorded in our ancient stories. It's no use to be condemning the modern world. No use launching into a diatribe against technology or an indictment of consumer culture or a tirade against Sunday shopping. The absence of God is not caused by those things. The absence of God is as old as the hills. Older. The Book of Job knows all about it:

Oh that I knew where I might find him . . .
Behold I go forward but he is not there;
And backward, but I cannot perceive him;
On the left hand I seek him but I cannot behold him;
I turn to the right hand, but I cannot see him . . .
For I am hemmed in by darkness,
And thick darkness covers my face. (Job 23:3ff)

Job – now there's a human being with problems. His health is rocky. He's got business failure. He's got family dynamics – what's left of his family. He's got emotional issues. But his biggest problem, the one he rails and rages and rebels against, is the absence. The godless, inscrutable absence.

I called you – no reply.

I was faithful – no reward.

I prayed – you hid your face.

I turned to the right and to the left – you just left.

Job is a decent human being but he is living in an absence, thick darkness upon his face. Millions of us decent human beings live in an absence. It's especially poignant for ministers, who have to keep talking as if God is here, all the while wondering how many people notice the thick darkness upon our faces.

Yet through all this, Job is discovering something about the living God. In the awful absence, Job has come face-to-face with the wildness of God.

That may be an odd way to say this – that God is wild. Theologians might use different language. They might say that God is sovereign. Or that God is inscrutable. Or that God is free. But I am saying that God is wild because that is the only clear way to convey that God is not domestic.

We call creatures "wild" when their ways are not our ways.

They have their own ways. The ways of the wild are not arbitrary or random or chaotic. They are not in contravention of all law. The wild ones have their own mysterious laws. They follow their own deep rhythms and patterns. They move to the sound of a music we cannot hear. Weather is wild in this sense, too. The wind blows where it wills. Thus it is with the Spirit: like the wind, said Jesus, wild like the wind.

The Book of Job is all about God who has never been tamed and who does not show up when summoned. It is all about, "Where is God when you need him?" About a good man who calls God to his side in a time of trial and is met with silence.

It's a terrible thing. I know a lot of people who, because of it, have abandoned faith. They've turned out the lights inside, locked the door and walked out alone into the night. They discard the Bible and its wild stories. They say it isn't true.

The truth is the Bible knows all about the absence of God. The Bible knows that God cannot be captured and trained. It knows that God is not, in this sense, available.

God says:

"You cannot see my face. . . ."

"My ways are not your ways. . . ."

"I am who I am and I will be what I am doing. . . ."

In the Book of Ezekiel, the presence of God is described as a glory or a radiant effulgence. The rabbinic word for this effulgence is *shekinah*. According to Ezekiel, the glory or the *shekinah* one day escapes out of the temple. Glory escapes and moves out over the city, over the wall, down through a ravine and out into the hills. It disappears. It is last seen heading east. Some presume it has gone all the way across the desert to Babylon. Imagine that for a moment if you were a loyal Israelite. Imagine the glory taking up with the Babylonians!

"I will be who I will be," says the Lord. "And I will go where I will go and I will hang with whom I will hang."

God will not be defined by Israel's religion. It's in the Bible. God will not be confined by Israel's nationalism. It's in the Bible. God will not be tamed by any religious tradition, no matter how loudly and how long that tradition booms out the divine name.

So if you feel that God is far away, you might be right. The glory might have slipped away while you were tending to the accoutrements of the temple. It has happened before. We are, most of the time, children of a dreadful absence. We are citizens of the wild kingdom, a kingdom we may belong to but which never belongs to us.

We cannot change any of this. But here are three things I think a person can do.

First, find a place in the church. Even if you are a mouse in the corner, find someplace where you can overhear the stories, especially the unlikely ones, the unmanageable ones, the untamed ones. They are most like God.

We don't go to church because God is present there. We go to church because in most of our experience, most of the time, God is absent. Oh, there is the rare and stunning moment of God's appearing in the landscape of a day, but it is a brief and passing moment. Most of our time is spent in the absence.

People think we're stupid to go to church. They say, "You're not aflame with faith and free. You're just going there out of habit: Sunday morning, sun comes up, having no will and no freedom of your own, you trudge off to church just like always."

Well, we're not that stupid. We are in the church because the community holds the faith and tells it and sings it when we cannot hold it and tell it and sing it for ourselves. The community remembers when we have forgotten. The community speaks the sacred name even when it has fallen silent on our lips. The community knows it's God's world even when we've become convinced that the world is a godforsaken wilderness of abandoned dreams and broken promises.

So find your place in the church where the tales of the wild God are remembered and told: God in the rain . . . God in a pregnancy . . . God in an execution. . . . Find a place in the church where the powerful hope is proclaimed that God shall come again, like a shoot from a great tree cut down, or like a rose blooming amid the cold of winter.

The second thing you can do is stop worrying about being well-adjusted. Beware the therapists who counsel adjustment to a godforsaken world. Job never accepted the absence. He railed, he raged, he rebelled. He refused the therapies offered to him. He would settle for no domestic imitation and neither must you. If you are not angry in a godforsaken world there's something wrong. You've achieved adjustment. You've imbibed the indifference that promotes itself as open-mindedness. You've come to tolerate everything – even the intolerable.

Canada may be a proud jurisdiction but it has an intolerable rate of violence against gay and lesbian people. Canadian politicians may be fond of saying that Canada is the best country in the world but the casinos are full and the churches are empty. Canada may be prosperous according to the national fiscal forecast, but it doesn't apply to any First Nations reserve I've ever been on. Don't adjust to these things. God may not be available but God is still God. When we shake a fist at the sky and shout, "God, where are you? How could you let this happen?" we are likely to hear the reply, "Indeed, where are you? How could *you*?"

Besides, remember Ezekiel and the glory? One day, it returned. Not that anyone was holding out much hope. After all, the glory had been gone for 19 years. People had grown accustomed to its absence. People had adjusted. But one day, out of nowhere, there it was, coming over the hills, headed for the temple.

How long has the glory been gone where you live? Days? Months? Years? Have you adjusted to the absence? Have you found stand-ins for the glory in the calculations of a successful life? Have you found substitutes for the glory in the techniques of a successful church? If you ever adjust to its being gone you won't have found reality, you'll have lost the wild gift of hope.

So be alert. You never know when the *shekinah* will be coming over the horizon – *like a thief in the night,* as Jesus said. (1 Thess. 5:2)

The third thing you can do is plant your young apple trees. This is what Martin Luther said he'd be doing if he knew it was his last day in the world – he'd be out planting life, planting young apple trees. Let God find you alive and at work, nurturing life when God chooses the time of appearing.

This is why God has given you moments to remember, when the glory drew near and you took off your shoes. So that you would know the way of life until God shall come again, like the rain, in God's own sweet time. Ethics is what we do while God is away.

But mark this. One day God will appear. Like that ragged figure Flannery O'Connor describes, the one that moves from tree to tree in the back of the mind. Or like the glory appearing over a distant hill. Or like a morsel of bread dipped in a cup. Or like a rose blooming amid the cold of winter when half-spent is the night.

Then you will know why you kept the faith – or more truthfully, why the faith kept you. On that day when the wild and holy one appears you can say, "Glory, I've been watching for you and waiting. I've been hoping you'd come. Roses are difficult here."

Dear George

The Very Rev. George Pidgeon, D.D., LL.D.
Bloor Street United Church
300 Bloor Street West
Toronto, ON
M5S 1W3

DEAR GEORGE,

I know this letter is not likely to reach you at Bloor Street United Church, but you were minister there for 33 years, and I thought it a place to start. Perhaps I should have addressed this to you at New Richmond on the Gaspé Coast where you grew up and where we have something in common. For six years I was minister on the New Carlisle pastoral charge, not far down the road from the farm where you were raised. Three of our children were born there.

This letter is written from my heart and bound for yours, whatever the address. Words coming from the heart must be received by the heart; hearing of the goodness of your heart gives me courage to write – that, and the respect in which you and your brother Leslie are held. Were you aware of the saying that used to go around the church? "There's no fighting the Pidgeons. Leslie is too clever, and George is too good."

Forgive me. I have ignored the courtesy of a formal greeting and addressed you in a familiar way. This is a characteristic of our age and is not meant to indicate any disrespect. Let me try again.

I greet you in Christ. In the strength of the communion of saints, I write across the chasm of the years to appeal for your solidarity of spirit and for your counsel.

That feels better.

There is something else we have in common. I serve The United Church of Canada as the 38th of its moderators. You were the first. How odd that you were elected moderator of the Presbyterian Church in Canada and a week later you were elected moderator of The United Church of Canada. Here in the Maritimes we would say that was some week.

This is a precarious time for the church we love – not bereft of hope, but a time of great diminishment and a certain desolation. You will understand my longing to speak with someone who accompanied The United Church of Canada through her tumultuous passage into life; someone who felt the pain and joy of our birth; someone who remembers why we are here. We are 80 years old and something in us is exhausted.

I am writing because I know you came to the idea of a United Church of Canada slowly, carefully, and then bravely. I believe you would want to know how things are with us now, and I hope you will understand.

Sometimes I wonder what was going through your mind in the Mutual Street Arena that day at the inaugural service of The United Church of Canada. I know that the order of service was the one you had long used at Bloor Street, but was it you who chose the processional hymn, The Church's One Foundation? Did your spine tingle when you came to the line that says, "Till with the vision glorious her longing eyes are blessed?"

I wonder what vision glorious your heart was seeing as you sang with the great crowd. I want you to know that in a way, much of what you must have dreamed has come to pass.

It wasn't without pain and it took time, but the wounds of the long struggle for union eventually healed. My grandmother was in her 20s when her congregation joined the new United Church. All her life she used to say, "We were Methodist, you know." My father, born in 1924, grew up in a congregation that was learning how to become a United Church. I was born the month after you retired. I have read accounts of the struggle for church union – how it was so hopeful in one place, so bitter in another. I have seen the scars, but I have no direct memory of it. My children don't really care much about that struggle. The wounds have healed too well.

After all these years we still encounter the old fault line though, the one between the socialists and the moralists (as they were called in your time). Even today, some of us understand evangelism as calling people to participate in building God's reign of social justice on earth. Some of us, on the other hand, understand evangelism as calling people to new birth in faith, thus building a better society one human life at a time. You will recognize that long-standing division. It hasn't changed much, but for the most part we don't use the word evangelism at all any more. There's something about it that embarrasses us.

I guess I still want to know about the vision glorious. There are allegations among us that the United Church has got away from the Gospel and into politics. The old question still rages: Is it the role of the General Council to lead congregations into public arenas many of them don't want to enter? Or is it the role of the General Council to represent the interests of congregations without whom the General Council would not exist at all?

Since its beginning, The United Church of Canada has implicated itself in the political life of the country and consequently in controversy. No one would know that better than you, George. Oddly enough, the evidence of General Council reports indicates that we were more radical in politics in your day than we are in mine. Still, I notice that two months after you were elected, you sent a letter to the whole church summoning members "to intercede for what our fathers called a revival of religion."

Revival of religion is a hard word to hear today, given our reduced prospects. Hard, and hopeful. Is revival of religion a part of the vision glorious, too?

At any rate, we both know that the United Church was born in ecumenism and raised on a social gospel. We grew up on a vision of Canada. The vision stands right up front in our founding document, the Basis of Union:

"It shall be the policy of the United Church to foster the spirit of unity in the hope that this sentiment of unity may in due time, so far as Canada is concerned, take shape in a church which may fittingly be described as national."

Could this be our founding charism? A national church? As a Presbyterian you would be quick to point out that it didn't say an established church, nor did it imply a church that is an acolyte of the government. Still, it did say "a church that may fittingly be described as national."

Is the vision glorious bound up somehow with Canada? My friend Ted Reeve says it is. He writes, "The goal of church union was to call into being a nation founded on the Christian values of democracy, mutuality and a redistributive ethic."

What do you think of this, George? Is it true? Were you and the many who worked for union seeking to call a nation into being? If you were, it is a vision stunning in its scale, and scandalous in its readiness to get into politics.

The evidence of wanting to bring a nation into being seems clear from the action of the 1932 General Council, when it formed a commission to "define those particular measures which must form the first steps toward a social order in keeping with the mind of Christ."

That kind of initiative has inspired and enabled The United

Church of Canada to make great contributions to the building of this country. For example, the United Church has been an important actor in the work of immigration that has so shaped the emerging Canada. Health care, pensions, employment insurance, human rights, the environment – the church has been a leader, often at considerable cost, in all these fields and in many others. I hope you know, George, that much of what you must have dreamed in the vision glorious has come to pass.

Furthermore, I could tell you countless stories of congregations who have been a great blessing to their communities and to their people. Through good times and bad they have persevered in the strength and the hope of the Gospel.

BUT I AM WRITING TO YOU because I need to tell you about some of the things that didn't work out so well.

The ministry among francophones in Quebec and other parts of Canada has not taken root in a way fitting to this country. The whole church has not risen to the opportunity and challenge of ministries in French, even as Canada was being transformed by ideals of bilingualism and biculturalism in the 1960s. This is an oddity and a disappointment for a church that longed to "fittingly be described as national."

The Indian residential schools seemed a progressive and generous initiative at the time, but they have left a legacy of bitterness and generations of disenfranchisement – the very things they were meant to address. It is true, the United Church has been a strong and faithful leader in addressing this national issue with integrity. But even as First Nations have been moving toward the centre of national consciousness and are beginning to acquire the land base and resources necessary to full partnership in the country, the presence of First Nations people in the life and work of the church remains on the margins. This, too, is an oddity and a disappointment for a church longing to be known as national.

Immigration and refugee work has always been near to our hearts and still is, but new Canadians have not found their way into the heart of the United Church in such a way as to transform the church as their presence has transformed the nation.

The same might be said of our own beloved young ones to whom we long to pass on the gifts of the Spirit and the power of the life in Christ but who are not with us in our churches. I think they sense that thing in the church, that exhaustion of the charism.

Will you understand if I say that the plan of bringing a nation into being is over – swept out of the way by a new world order and burdened by the weight of unrequited dreams?

Our last great venture in ecumenism ended 30 years ago when the plan of union with the Anglican Church failed. Our financial strength peaked and began a slow decline at about the same time. After doubling our membership in the generation after church union, we now count the same number of members as we did when you were elected in 1925.

Canada is a secular utopia now, built on the pillars of human rights and multiculturalism. Canada is a beautiful dream, really. It is a critical experiment in the contemporary world and a hope-bearer for the planet. But I suspect you would agree that a secular, rights-based, multicultural utopia, for all its strengths, is not our Gospel.

I am asking your counsel, George, on how we might keep faith with your commitment to this country and how might we live again by what you called a revival of religion. It all seems so out of reach. Our circumstance is reduced in almost every congregation and mission. That's the truth and it hurts.

At least we know this: the truth is the only thing that can heal the very wounds it inflicts. The truth takes us down deep, down to the bottom, and there it opens the door. It could be that the vision glorious is still alive but that we must perceive it now from a different place, a lower place, a deeper place. We haven't forgotten what it is to be born in ecumenism and raised on the social gospel, but we are being driven down by the Spirit. When the Spirit drives you down it widens out your heart – down and out into a new work of faith. Down and out.

HERE'S WHAT I'M DREAMING, George, and I am writing to ask if the dream upholds your best hopes.

Instead of instructing the country on what to become, perhaps we are being moved by the Spirit to become something ourselves. We can no longer expect Canada to listen when we tell it how to behave and what to believe in. We can do something better. We can become in ourselves what we long for the country to be. Thus the saying, "You can't always make a great work of art but you can always be one." If the effort bears fruit, The United Church of Canada will be respected not for what we say but for what we are.

This is why I look for the day when francophones are welcomed to a place at the heart and on the lips of the church; when First Nations peoples stand and speak among us as founders, teachers and leaders who are opening another way; when new Canadians are instrumental in shaping a changing church for a changing country; when young people don't have to go away to dream their dreams anymore; and when our elders in the faith are accorded an honoured place.

For the church, this would be an act of faith on a life-changing scale. It would require the reordering of our ecclesiology and of our economy and the learning of languages. The vision glorious would have to be shared and passed among different hands and new hearts. It would be a difficult passage. It would take a generation and we would surely not accomplish it perfectly. No generation ever has. But George, we belong to The United Church of Canada and to her founding charism – a church that may fittingly be described as national – and we would keep faith with you in this.

I am not suggesting that the church should imitate the country. Surely the church leads best by being a living example of an alternative community. We would have to learn a way of being together that is not simply a means of brokering competing interests, rights and cultures. The United Church of Canada welcomes diversity because living organisms thrive on diversity, and so will we. But the statement of purpose you and your colleagues wrote into the Basis of Union keeps coming to mind: "It shall be the policy of the United Church to foster the spirit of unity in the hope that this sentiment of unity may in due time, so far as Canada is concerned, take shape in a church which may fittingly be described as national."

Unity – we know it requires diversity because genuine unity is made of diverse constituents. Otherwise our unity degenerates into uniformity by assimilation. It requires an essential attitude of respect and a responsibility to live out of our common humanity. We have so much to learn about the unity of the body in which each has an honoured place, to which each contributes and to which all belong.

I hope that the church can arrive at an alternative meaning for the word "national" as it appears in our founding statement of purpose. In its present form, the word holds echoes of empire and imposes arbitrary boundaries on the natural contours and indigenous cultures of God's good earth. The church, of all communities, ought to know that it is good to love your country, but there is no reason that love should stop at the border. The United Church has a rich history of partnership around the world, partnership that has taught us that borders cannot contain love. Canada, at its best, knows this too.

I believe that in every village, town and city in Canada there needs to be a community of people, people of the United Church, who are willing to become in themselves what they long for their communities and their country to be. We will need leaders who are church planters, who have the courage and the vision to nurture communities of faith that are an alternative to the empires that demand and assume our allegiance.

I know some say we should turn back to that vision of the church as a demanding and rewarding company of the saved. I know they say that we have brought our sorrows upon ourselves because we have turned away from our Gospel. But I am convinced that we must go ahead.

We must set out again toward the incarnation of Christ. I know we'll never be true to our Gospel by becoming a rights-based utopia grounded in the ideology of multiculturalism. That's not who we are. We are a body-based community grounded in Christ crucified and risen – the door at the bottom of the world.

We are not on the way to becoming a successful church; we are on the way to being changed into the likeness of Christ as it seems good to the Spirit to do. That is to say, healing and sustenance are our work. Crossing boundaries of alienation between people is our way. Grace, forgiveness and new life are the gifts by which we live. It is daunting to have to create alternative communities in the political and cultural marketplace of Canada, not to mention having to do it in the ruins of the first incarnation of the vision glorious. It requires of us much more courage, love and vision than we suspect we have. But where else will we grow, except where we are planted, and why would we set out to do for our country what we have not been able to do for ourselves?

GEORGE, THE STORY YOU TELL about your first day of school is coming to mind – how at the age of four you set out from home to walk to the schoolhouse. You only got as far as your uncle Ben's barn before turning back that first day. But the next day you tried again. Eventually you made it to school and from school to a wide new world. I think that's how it is. In 80 years we've come as far as Uncle Ben's barn. In the morning we will set out for our destiny again.

Wherever this finds you, my treasured colleague and friend in Christ, I hope it finds you in good spirit. If it finds you at Bloor

Street, please greet the sisters and brothers in Christ there. If you are at the farm on the coast, please indulge me by taking a walk in one of those fields of clover in the spring of the year; inhale deeply the scent carried on the breeze from the Baie des Chaleurs and look up at the wide blue sky. You'll think you are in heaven.

Blessings in Christ to whom we, with the whole church, belong. Please be assured of my gratitude for your founding work and my promise to do all I can in the strength of God to keep faith with the vision glorious.

I remain faithfully yours in the hope of your reply.

Rt. Rev. Peter Short
Moderator
The United Church of Canada

God Is in the Building

ONE WHO HAS STRUGGLED ALL THESE YEARS to live by a law of just deserts hates the sound of grace. I serve the church and I've worked hard to preserve the sanctity of the holy place. I hate to see the rules broken. I hate to see the overturning of the tables that guard the entrance and the door to the holy place standing wide open. Anybody could walk right in – free as you please. Grace is a security threat.

Guilt has always worked for me. Guilt has allowed me at least the satisfaction of condemning myself from some patch of high moral ground. I can give up a lot but don't ask me to forego my guilt. I'd rather hold on to it than fall into the hands of forgiveness. Guilt is the last stronghold of pride.

There is an oddity among us religious people. Often what galls us most deeply is nothing less than the prodigal love of the Living One. Theologian Karl Barth observed that many people go to church to make their last stand against God. So I'm not the only one. There are a lot of us in the church who, when it comes right down to it, are making a principled last stand against Jesus the forgiver, the opener of the entrance, the one who thinks that feeding one another, forgiving and healing one another, are the most important things in all the world. We'd rather settle for anxiety than abandon ourselves to faith.

Sometimes when I'm trying to hold the church together (not to mention myself), I suspect that the conflict and intellectual dissonance I feel is a sign: not that God has left the building, but that God is in the kitchen stirring the pot. I would dismiss such a thought as whistling in the dark were it not for the 20th chapter of Jeremiah. In that chapter the prophet drags up every unhappy circumstance in order to justify the end of the relationship with the Living One. It is an attempt to get God out of the building, but it fails. Every time Jeremiah rises to leave, having declared the place empty, God shows up.

To begin with, in Jeremiah's way of thinking the struggle is hardly fair: *O Lord, Thou hast enticed me and I was enticed. Thou art stronger than I and thou hast prevailed.* (Jer. 20:7a)

It may be the reluctant believers like Jeremiah who at the last become the strongest. They have battled and lost. They have given excuses and run away. Yet, in spite of every effort to the contrary, they end up helplessly loving the Lord. They are enticed by the one who is stronger. C.S. Lewis described himself in this way – the most reluctant of converts, surprised by joy. *Thou hast prevailed.* Some of us just can't walk away.

Furthermore, for the prophet nothing is paying off: *The Word of the Lord has become for me a derision and a reproach all day long.* (Jer.20:9)

He is ridiculed and ridicule is a bitter potion to swallow. Sticks and stones break bones but names hurt too. Still, if it is true that self-respect is anxiety's substitute for grace, ridicule may in the end become a powerful medicine in healing – a kind of homeopathy of the spirit. Since he can't seem to leave, even ridicule makes the relationship stronger. An apostle of Jesus would one day make the same point:

Who will separate us from the love of Christ? Will hardship, or distress, or persecution, or famine, or nakedness, or peril, or sword?. . . I am convinced that neither death nor life, nor angels, nor rulers, nor things pres-

ent, *nor things to come, nor height, nor depth nor anything else in all creation, will be able to separate us from the love of God in Christ Jesus our Lord.* (Rom. 8:35,38)

The prophet has become sick of the difficult path he has been walking with God but at the same time he finds that he cannot turn back: *If I say I will not mention Him or speak any more in His name, there is in my heart a burning fire shut up in my bones and I am weary with holding it in and I cannot.* (Jer.20 9)

I think I know what this is – the burning fire in the heart and in the bones. Sometimes I can hold in the burning fire, quite effectively actually, especially when danger is involved. But inevitably it makes me sick to do so – sick of what I become when I try to fill God's place with strategic manoeuvres or even with my own best self.

And what ever happened to the promise of peace that passeth understanding? *The Lord is with me as a dread warrior.* (Jer.20:11a)

The presence of the dread warrior will not be escaped or appeased or domesticated. The writer of Psalm 139 had praised the presence that preceded and awaited him even in the uttermost parts of the sea. Jeremiah resents it.

The reluctant servant of God says he would be happier if he hadn't been born, as might many of us be if we hadn't been born again: *Cursed be the day on which I was born. Why did I come forth from the womb to see toil and sorrow and spend my days in shame?* (Jer. 20:14)

Why did I come forth from the womb? God knows. God knows why and that's precisely the problem.

It would all be much simpler if the disappointments and the conflicts and the intellectual dissonance were signs that God has left the building. But at a deeper level I know that such things are tormenting signs that a presence is calling for health and new life. Or, to use the older word, salvation. God is in the building. In fact, God is in the kitchen stirring the pot.

Is there no escaping this God-haunted house? If it weren't for Jeremiah I'd be out of here. Come to think of it, better add the Psalmist and Paul as well. If it weren't for them I'd be gone. Actually, there does seem to be considerable precedent for this predicament I find myself in. Moses made excuses. Peter ran away. Mary got impatient when things went badly. And of course there is the one who suffered the ultimate intellectual dissonance and who passed through the conflict that claimed his life – and set it free in the world.

Maybe I am walking an old and well-travelled path after all. Maybe I am once again the prodigal: sick of home . . . homesick . . . home. My people have known this all along, yet somehow it is a knowledge that must be struggled through anew in each precious life – how hard it is and how good it is to live in this old house. Thank God. I think perhaps I'll go into the kitchen to see who's at the table and what's on the stove.

Conclusion

THE THINGS I HAVE SPOKEN OF in this book have been sighted in the nest of Christian tradition. It is a demanding tradition – beautiful and difficult. In ways with which you are familiar, the Christian tradition is a damaged nest, as in some sense we all are damaged. Still, it is a nest that cradles tiny hatchlings of hope. In some way that's all we are – tiny hatchlings of hope. I wanted to point to that.

In the introduction I wrote that you don't have life, life has you: "This is all it really means to be a believer. It is to realize that you've been snatched out of oblivion by life." I hope that somewhere in these lines or between them you will have realized. I hope you will have caught a glimpse of the unmanageable Spirit by which you live – unmanageable because the Spirit by which you live is not really yours to own. It is the Spirit we have called holy.

The Spirit in every one of us is at once a wild presence that bears us away and an intimate presence that speaks to us of a home we scarcely know. I think that's what Jesus taught us – freedom and love.

I wanted to tell you in these pages that the price Jesus paid for hope and the price we will pay to walk with him is not too great. It is the price of freedom, of love and of new life. If freedom, love and new life matter more than anything else, the price is not too great.

Most of what I have written comes from the past. It has been learned as history or remembered in the living of my days. The past is how we understand ourselves and make our lives into meaning. We make our meaning only when the bewildering present has left.

But there is another meaning. It is the one that beckons us from tomorrow. It is time now, as these pages come to an end, to look with Jesus into what might lie in the uncharted landscape beyond today.

Jesus and his disciples left that place and went on through Galilee. Jesus did not want anyone to know where he was, because he was teaching his disciples: The Son of Man will be handed over to those who will kill him. Three days later, however, he will rise to life. (Mk. 9:30,31)

It would not be a good thing to know the future. If we knew, everything would be inevitable. Who wants to live in an inevitable world? There would be no freedom. All would be laid out for you in advance. Imagine a conversation like this as you go out the door in the morning: "I'm on my way, my love. Oh no! I'll be running into Paddy at lunchtime. You know, my old school buddy I haven't seen in 25 years? We're going to have a clichéd conversation about what a small world it is. I'll be home at 6:23. Oh, and by the way, I'll be forgetting to pick up those stamps you wanted."

Do you think Jesus knew the future?

The Son of Man will be handed over to those who will kill him. Three days later, however, he will rise to life.

I don't think he knew. Or maybe he knew in the way a young couple knows when they stand at the front of the church and speak their promises: "for better or for worse . . . for richer, for poorer . . . in sickness and in health." Maybe Jesus knew that whatever might be out there ahead, some of it will be in joy and some will be in sorrow.

Maybe Jesus knew the future the way an old man knows it as he looks across the river and murmurs as if he's talking to the clear blue sky: "We'll meet again, don't know where, don't know when. . . ." Maybe Jesus knew that whatever river there is to cross, the heart will go on loving and hoping in the face of the inevitable. Maybe that's largely what being human is – living full, in full view of the evidence.

The Son of Man will be handed over to those who will kill him.

Whatever he knew, Jesus saw that there would come a terrible cost.

Three days later, however, he will rise to life.

Whatever he knew, Jesus saw that there would be a victory – a victory of life.

That is the Jesus story by which we live. There is a terrible cost and buried deep in the terrible cost there is a victory, which is the passage into new life.

We don't know the future exactly but we try to prepare for it nonetheless. We are like the man who was given advice as he prepared to enter the hospital for an operation: "Before undergoing a surgical operation arrange your temporal affairs. You may live."

That's it. In Christ you may live. But oh my, it's going to be costly. That's what the friends of Jesus were finding out that day when he talked with them about the future.

They wanted a high place in the economy of tomorrow. In fact, they had just asked for the honoured places on the right hand and on the left in the kingdom. Jesus said they could have a high place all right, and the cost of such a high place would be all their status. *He who would be greatest among you must be the least and the servant of all.* (Mk. 9:35) So what will an important place cost you? All your importance. They began to see that the victory is dear.

What will happiness cost you? You will not even know what happiness is until you can feel the sorrow of another person. There will be no happiness until you've seen the world through tears and walked in the landscape of devastation. *Happy are you who weep,* said Jesus (Lk. 6:21b). Happy are you who mourn. It costs everything.

There is no true victory that does not come out of the loss of what you had been. That's the Jesus story. We are being taught such things by people among us who belong to the victory of Christ even as they are dragged through the defeats of the world they live in. Life is a victory but you don't always win.

On the other hand, victory that preserves everything you had been is no victory at all. It's just winning. Winning is not the Jesus story. It is some other story.

Winners create losers. Pilate was a winner. Jesus was a loser. By the reckoning of winners, Terry Fox was a loser too. He failed to make it all the way across the country in his epic Marathon of Hope. He didn't win because the cancer returned in his lungs and he had to stop in those great hills north of Superior. Terry Fox didn't make it. But on second thought, I guess it depends on what you think making it means.

The Son of Man will be handed over to those who will kill him. Three days later, however, he will rise to life.

The victory of Christ costs everything, even the "you" you cling to. Then, on the other side of loss, there is a rising. It is a mysterious, frightening and inexplicable rising. It may be scarcely recognizable at first, and the telling of it will seem a foolishness and the speech will be in hesitant whispers. But it will be there nonetheless and the rising will name you a new creation.

This is more or less why Rabbi Simcha Bunam said, "Keep two truths in your pocket and take them out according to the need of the moment. Let one be: For my sake the world was created. And the other: I am dust and ashes."

Any life can be a victory and will be a victory when it is lived in Christ. This is the terrible mystery that will drive you out into the wilderness. It is the same mystery that will lead you home.

Selected Readings

For The Time Being by Annie Dillard (Vintage) 1999

The Inner Voice of Love by Henri Nouwen (Image) 1998

Prophet of Orthodoxy: The Wisdom of G.K. Chesterton by G.K. Chesterton and Russell Sparkes (Fount) 1997

The Habit of Being: Letters of Flannery O'Connor by Flannery O'Connor (Vintage) 1988

Wishful Thinking: A Theological ABC by Frederick Buechner (HarperSanFrancisco) 1993

Mother's Ruin: A History of Gin by John Basil Watney (Owen) 1976

Living the Truth in a World of Illusions by William Sloane Coffin (Harper & Row) 1985

Claiming the Social Passion by Ted Reeve (The United Church of Canada) 1999

Endnotes

Scripture quotations unless otherwise noted are from the New Revised Standard Version, © copyright 1989 by the Division of Christian Education of the National Council of the Churches of Christ in the United States of America. Used by permission. All rights reserved.

Scripture quotations in the Conclusion are from the Good News Bible, © copyright 1994 published by the Bible Societies/HarperCollins Publishers Ltd., UK Good News Bible © copyright American Bible Society 1966, 1971, 1976, 1992. Used by permission.

Scripture quotations in "Wild Roses" are from the Revised Standard Version, © copyright 1952 [2nd edition, 1971] by the Division of Christian Education of the National Council of the Churches of Christ in the United States of America. Used by permission. All rights reserved.

Every reasonable effort has been made to contact the holders of copyright for materials quoted in this work. The publisher will gladly receive information that will enable it to rectify any inadvertent errors or omissions in subsequent editions.

Outside Eden was edited by Muriel Duncan and Donna Sinclair; copyedited by David Wilson; additional research by Fran Oliver; proofreading by Caley Moore.

Cover and interior design: Ross Woolford
Cover photo: Science Photo Library
Back cover photo: David Smith/M.D.S. Photography

Printed in Canada by Transcontinental Printing